America
FOR

Simple Things Each of Us Can Do
to Make Our Country Better

A FOR America

Simple Things Each of Us Can Do to Make Our Country Better

☆ ☆

Forewords by Presidents

George H. W. Bush
AND William Jefferson Clinton

Written by SACHA ZIMMERMAN

Reader's Digest

The Reader's Digest Association, Inc.
Pleasantville, New York

A READER'S DIGEST BOOK

Copyright @ 2006 The Reader's Digest Association, Inc.

All rights reserved. Unauthorized reproduction, in any manner, is prohibited.

Reader's Digest is a registered trademark of
The Reader's Digest Association, Inc.

Library of Congress Cataloging-in-Publication Data
For America : simple things each of us can do to make our country better.
    p. cm.
  ISBN 0-7621-0829-0 (hardcover)
  1. United States—Social conditions—1980- I. Reader's Digest Association.
HN59.2.F67 2006
303.48'4097309045—dc22   2006022909

Address any comments about *For America* to:
The Reader's Digest Association, Inc.
Editor in Chief
Reader's Digest Books
Reader's Digest Road
Pleasantville, NY 10570-7000

For more Reader's Digest products and information,
visit our website **RD.com**

Printed in the United States of America

1 3 5 7 9 10 8 6 4 2

A special thank you to the Honorable Melvin R. Laird—
the friend of presidents, of Reader's Digest,
and all of America.

Contents

George H. W. Bush

41ST PRESIDENT OF THE UNITED STATES

In our relatively short history as Americans, we have always been a country of doers and risk takers. After all, every single one of our ancestors left the comforts of another life in another land to seek greater freedom and opportunity in this land we now share.

There is no better example than our Founding Fathers, who took on the mightiest empire in the world to procure our freedom. Yet we often forget that they were just ordinary citizens—farmers, shopkeepers, housewives, laborers—who wanted the same things then that we want now: opportunities to better themselves through education and employment; a safe, secure environment in which to live and raise their families; the right to seek good fortune and happiness. They didn't set out to change the course of history; they just wanted to correct some problems they saw and could not tolerate.

Many of you have heard the story of the Frenchman Alexis de Tocqueville, who came here in the 1830s. His goal was to figure out this mysterious new country called the United States. He seemed most intrigued by Americans' odd habit of getting together and finding solutions to common problems. "It is impossible to prevent men from assembling, getting excited together and forming sudden passionate resolves," he wrote in his book *Democracy in America*. He seemed amazed by this phenomenon and declared it a uniquely American characteristic.

From the beginning, our presidents have considered it part of their job to remind all Americans of their responsibility as citizens. That is exactly what Thomas Jefferson meant when he wrote, "I'm too old to plant trees for my own gratification, I shall do it for my posterity." Abraham Lincoln challenged his countrymen when he said, "To sin by silence when they should protest makes cowards of men." A half century later, Teddy Roosevelt reminded us, "Much has been given to us, and much is rightly expected of us. We have duties to others, and duties to ourselves, and we can shirk neither."

Modern-day presidents have been just as persistent in trying to instill good citizenship. I still like to talk about "a thousand points of light" when I ask everyone to remember that any definition of a successful life must include service to others. My successor, Bill Clinton, put it this way: "We need a spirit of community, a sense that we are all in this together. If we have no sense of community, the American dream will wither." Our current president was even more direct. In his first inaugural address, George W. Bush said, "I ask you to be citizens—citizens, not spectators ... responsible citizens, building communities of service and a nation of character."

But perhaps the best-known quote on the topic came from John F. Kennedy, who simply told all Americans to ask not what their country could do for them but what they could do for their country. When he spoke those words in 1961, our nation was facing unusually great challenges. Our safety and security were under threat from the rising tide of Communism and its leading proponents, the former Soviet Union and Cuba. The nascent and often brutal Civil Rights Movement had the people of our nation deeply and often angrily at odds. Early stumbles in a high-stakes race to the Moon made us question our ability to remain the scientific and technical leader of the world. And the erection of the Berlin Wall forced us to reconsider our leadership role in a world of nations.

But many Americans took President Kennedy's words to heart, set aside their fears, and decided to become more active citizens. The result was a new chapter in America's history that many believe was even greater than that which came before it. A national Peace Corps was started, the United States landed on the Moon before any other nation, we entered an age of unprecedented equality and rights for all, American entrepreneurs began to create and define the new technologies of our time, and the Communist threat, the Soviet Union, and the Berlin Wall all crumbled.

But despite all the remarkable technological, social, and political progress, today we face new problems and challenges. The threats that face our mighty nation come not from looming superpowers but from rootless, stateless foes who skulk in shadows. Once again, heartfelt issues regarding race, life, and human rights have us deeply divided. And a fast-changing world has us wondering what our future role should be, not just politically but also economically and ideologically. And yet, as surely as the power of our citizenry changed the course of history so many times in the past, our citizens—that is, you and me—still have remarkable power that's more than adequate to change the world yet again. Our greatness as a country is inextricably bound to our greatness as a people.

At its bare minimum, citizenship means merely paying your taxes and obeying the law. At its zenith, however, citizenship creates the kind of momentum that can shelter thousands of hurricane victims, stop questionable legislation dead in its tracks, cause revolution in how health care is delivered, and even change how the world perceives us. Outstanding citizenship happens quietly all over America every time a meal is delivered to an elderly neighbor, a student is mentored, or a letter is written to the editor. Citizenship is an attitude, an approach that says, "I want a good life not just for me and my family, but for all the people with whom I share this land."

I've had the privilege of seeing such citizenship in action throughout my life. My dad was very active in town politics when I was growing up, and after a long day at work in the city, he would ride the train home and try to figure out what to do about potholes in our suburb. I still remember, when Barbara and I were just starting out in Midland, Texas, the great satisfaction that came after a group of us managed to raise the money and open the first YMCA. Ten years later, when I was a congressman from Houston, I had an annoying constituent who wrote me letter after letter after letter complaining about this and that and giving me unsolicited advice. You know what? I listened, and we actually became friends. Then, as president, one of my favorite jobs was to award the daily Points of Light, recognizing ordinary citizens who did extraordinary things every single day.

On their own, acts of good citizenship may seem small, even trivial. But don't believe for a moment that they don't matter. What if the child you are mentoring or coaching grows up to become a great business leader? What if your letter to the editor sparks the imagination of your state legislator? What if your watchful eye on your neighborhood stops a crime from occurring? Sometimes, we may never fully know the impact we have had on the world; at other times, the results of our actions may be as palpable as a heartbeat.

As this book points out, optimism and hope are never naive, and skepticism and debate need not be negative. All are crucial components of good citizenship. What can hurt us as a people are the extremes: pure idealism that doesn't acknowledge the realities of our modern world or the opinions of others, and pure cynicism that dismisses all ideas and hope without thought. In actuality, the pulse of American culture is imbued with both confidence and debate. It is up to all of us to maintain that vigor and make our nation and world even richer and more dynamic.

Though sometimes the issues that concern a nation—from terrorism and immigration to the economy and the environment—seem too big for just one person to affect, the truth is that you can always make a difference. When you feel beleaguered by events or even by the evening news, and you think, "What can I possibly do?" this book will offer you ways to empower yourself. Each of us can tackle the weightiest of issues; each of us can do our part to ensure a vibrant country. Each of us can ask ourselves what our forefathers did so many years ago: "What can we do for America?"

William Jefferson Clinton

42ND PRESIDENT OF THE UNITED STATES

In my first inaugural address, I said that
there is nothing wrong with America that cannot be
cured by what is right with America.

I am more convinced of that today than ever before, and more convinced that every citizen can help change our country for the better and build a stronger nation for our children.

Americans can always be counted on to respond to adversity or crisis. In the aftermath of Hurricane Katrina, former President George H. W. Bush and I tried to help the Gulf Coast to rebuild. We were inspired by the tremendous outpouring of generosity from people around the country, as huge numbers of volunteers streamed into the Gulf Coast to search for survivors, to provide emergency food and medical assistance, and to help cope with the challenges that lay ahead. Many more did what they could without leaving their communities. Those who could spare the room took in New Orleans residents whose houses had been destroyed. Schools opened their doors to displaced students. People held drives to gather supplies that could be sent to those in need. Countless others contributed what they could to relief funds.

We must also work to foster a commitment to this kind of service in more normal times. There are many constant challenges facing our country. Problems like poverty, inadequate school systems, homelessness, increasing childhood obesity and other health problems also require the attention and involvement of dedicated citizens.

One of the proudest moments of my Administration was the creation of AmeriCorps, which offers funding for college to citizens who spend a year or two serving in communities across America. During my Presidency, nearly 200,000 Americans took advantage of this opportunity to help others and improve their futures—more than have served in the entire forty-year history of the Peace Corps. Now more than 400,000 have served. They do vital work, teaching students to read, building homes, working with seniors, and immunizing children.

It's tremendously gratifying to see a culture of public service growing in our nation's young people, but the opportunity and obligation to serve extends to citizens of all ages. Age and experience enable people to help in many different ways.

My Foundation has a program called the Urban Enterprise Initiative. It offers technical and managerial support to small businesses and entrepreneurs. In Harlem, where my office is located, an economic revitalization is under way that has brought new opportunities to the community, but new challenges to existing businesses. So we organized pro bono teams of consultants from Booz Allen Hamilton, graduate business students from New York University's Stern School of Business, and professionals from a number of other partner organizations, including the National Black MBA Association to help participating businesses become more efficient and increase their profitability. After the teams do their work, volunteer business mentors recruited in cooperation with Inc. Magazine continue to work with growing enterprises.

I'm just as proud of these volunteers as the young AmeriCorps members. It's not necessary to take a year off to dedicate yourself exclusively to public service. You can use your existing skills, just like the participants in the Urban Enterprise Initiative, to help others after work or on weekends. Whether you work in IT, construction, or health care, your time and your skills can benefit your community.

Carroll Quigley, one of my college professors, taught that our civilization is the greatest in the world because our people have always believed that the future can be better than the present and that each of us has a personal responsibility to make it so. *For America* lays out a number of ways that you can fulfill your personal responsibility—and celebrate your right—to build a better future and keep our nation strong. You may not agree with every position advocated in this book. I don't, but I hope that reading about others' commitments to citizen service will inspire you to do your part.

Nurturing a Stronger
Family

We are all so busy—not just working adults, but *all* of us. Our children play in organized sports leagues, take music lessons, practice for school plays, enter science fairs, cram for college entrance exams, juggle play dates, and need rides everywhere. Seniors work, volunteer, travel, go to the doctor, and otherwise fill their time far more robustly than in previous generations. To top it all off, we haven't seen members of our extended families in years because they live across the country and, well, they are just so busy, too.

The result of all this busy-ness, if we're not careful, can be weaker families, and that's not good—neither for you and your children nor for your country. If America is a reflection of its people, then people are reflections of

their families. When you nurture your family, you are also nurturing the future of our nation.

Remember, your children are more than a collection of report cards and extracurricular achievements. They are the continuation of the values, traits, and priorities that are most important to you, your spouse, and those who came before you. This transfer of values doesn't happen on its own, though. It takes lots of talks, lots of shared moments, and lots of love. Likewise, your parents, grand-parents, uncles, and aunts aren't just people who are old. They are the wise elders of your families, to whom you owe much. So take a breath and recall why you love these people who breeze in and out of your home. Then take the time to nurture your family.

- ONE -

Eat Dinner Together

Dining together as a family used to be an institution, a practice so common as to be taken for granted.

But nowadays, many overworked parents and overscheduled kids have let family dinners slide to the point where they have become relics of our childhoods, mere memories of parents yelling, "Diiiiinnner!" from the front porch.

Remember feeding the dog your lima beans? Or keeping your elbows off the table? Or never seeming to have a good answer for "So what did you learn in school today?" It may seem like just so much nostalgia, but the truth is that family dinners are part of the fabric that binds families together.

Dinnertime means learning how to eat in peace with brothers and sisters, how to help prepare and clean up, how to ask for seconds and not grab, how to ask politely to leave the table, and even how to eat properly with utensils. At dinner, kids can listen to their parents discuss issues that arose for them at work and even learn how Mom or Dad resolved a problem. And parents can find out about their kids: who their friends and favorite teachers are and why one child wants to take ballet and another wants to quit the football team. In other words, dinner is a daily family meeting where you sit down for a while and check in with the most important people in your life.

The benefits are even greater for children. Studies show that children who regularly have sit-down dinners with their parents get better grades; are less likely to be involved with drugs; and eat healthier, more nutritious meals.

Of course, none of this means that times haven't changed. With soccer practices, cello lessons, and school play rehearsals, life is more hectic than ever. This being America, however, entrepreneurs are doing all they can to solve the problem of having too little time to put together a healthy dinner.

• There's hardly a supermarket that doesn't offer fresh-roasted chicken, a salad bar, a soup bar, and a deli counter filled with ready-to-eat entrées and side dishes.

• Dinnerplanner.com is a great source of tips on how to make a healthy dinner quickly. The site provides menus and shopping lists and even rates which meals make for easy cleanup.

• Dinner A'Fare is a fast-growing franchise that offers a full-service kitchen in which customers can prepare 12 meals in just 2 hours. The business specializes in fresh ingredients; the staff does the slicing, dicing, and prep, so you can just stop at a meal station and start cooking. Check it out at DinnerAFare.com.

• Gourmetgroceryonline.com provides premade fresh meals delivered straight to your door.

- TWO -

Gather the Extended Family

Once we spoke of the deep roots of family. Today, children seem more like the seeds of a dandelion, scattering across the country at the first breeze of adulthood.

So many American small towns have seen their populations—and hopes—decline as their young residents depart for the cities. Young people are attending college at record-breaking rates, and convenient travel options have made it possible for people to live just about anywhere.

Does this dissolution of tightly knit family clusters hurt the fabric of America? Will a new generation of kids grow up in virtual estrangement from cousins? Will family traditions be forgotten? Absolutely not—if you take action. Families are proving over and over that it's not necessary for members to live near each other in order to stay emotionally close. Modern technology makes long-distance communication easier than ever, and with a little work, an occasional gathering of the tribe can work magic in mending the damage of distance.

Family gatherings not only provide connective tissue between generations, they also provide a way to preserve the family narrative and identity. We are not just homogeneous members of a modern popular culture. We are the heirs of immigrants; we are the descendants of moonshine makers and gold diggers; we are the children of survivors and veterans; we are the relatives of slaves and nobility.

So every five years or so, reconnect with that personal history and teach the new generations about the sacrifices made and wars fought, the financial odds beaten, the jokes only your clan finds funny, the other nationalities and traditions that hold a special place in your DNA. Create a legacy with a family reunion and connect your family to roots that have wound their way for thousands of years just to get to you.

Plus, picnics are fun! Here are ideas to get you started.

• First, contact everyone in your family for whom you have a phone number, e-mail address, or street address. Ask these folks to help you expand your list.

• Select a site that's big enough to accommodate your clan in an area that offers affordable lodging for out-of-towners.

• Plan activities for the big day. Set up storytelling circles, memorabilia stands, and group photo stations; put together a family recipe book or a family tree; make baby-picture name tags; host a family talent show; and of course, give out awards.

For more ideas, check out Family-Reunion.com and remember to nurture ties to the past—and have a blast!

THREE

Teach Your Children About Real Life

We all hope that the values that are important to each
of us are passed along to our children.

Often, however, that hope is challenged by a deluge of pop-
culture messages, peer pressure, and overscheduled lives that
leave little time for good counsel or reflection. It's easy to forget that learning values and character at home is as important
as any schoolwork or extracurricular activity.

In the real world of jobs and career, people are judged by two
standards: their professional skills and their personal traits.
While grade school, high school, and college can teach skills
and proficiency, it's up to parents to teach children the attributes that make for success in the real world—diligence, a
cooperative attitude, creativity, optimism, assertiveness, and
honesty. Schools—particularly colleges—don't focus on these
issues. That's the job of the parents, so take the assignment

seriously. Send your kids into the world ready to handle not only the tasks of life but also its hurdles, social obstacles, and frustrations with finesse and character.

You really can't start soon enough. After all, children need personal integrity and morals as much as any adult. Bullies will always be around, tasks won't always be assigned fairly, the good guys won't always win, petty concerns will often trump issues of substance, and money won't always be in ample supply. Exposing children to the harsher realities of life isn't cruel; giving them that experience and coaching them through it is part and parcel of raising kids to have courage, resilience, and honor.

Do this exercise: Write down the 5 to 10 most important messages you want your children to truly understand by the time they enter the real world. Then think through how to teach these crucial lessons. Talking to your kids should be only part of the plan. Letting them witness integrity in action—through your own behavior, by watching documentaries about great people together, or even by visiting a courtroom—is the strongest way to impart the message. By identifying the specific attributes you would like to see in your children, you're more likely to reinforce those characteristics. So make a point of it. After all, if you don't teach your children integrity, who will?

- FOUR -

Be a One-Television Household

How addicted has America become to television? The
numbers are disturbing but hardly surprising.

- In the typical American household, the television is on for
more than 7 hours a day.
- The average American child spends more time watching TV
than attending school.
- By age 70, the average person will have spent 7 to 10 years
of his life watching television.

Just think of all the other things we could be doing to
improve ourselves and the country—bike riding, volunteering
at a soup kitchen, reading, gardening, playing—instead of sitting frozen in front of TV shows that are often violent, often
cruel, and often meaningless.

How troublesome has it become? Increasingly, the television
has moved from the family room into the kitchen and into
children's bedrooms, often acting as a baby-sitter or substitute

friend. Americans now average 2.4 TVs per household, according to the last census. And the effects are pernicious: Studies show that television can contribute to poor grades, obesity, and sleep and behavior problems in children. But that's not all: TV violence is epidemic. Before finishing grade school, the average child will witness about 8,000 murders depicted on TV. Pundits and scientists can debate whether such viewing changes how children act, but let common sense prevail here. Do we really want our children to see this much violence and hatred, especially in the name of entertainment?

Taking TV out of their bedrooms is a first step toward limiting the amount of television your children watch. Plus, in a one-set home where the TV is in a central location, it's easier for parents to monitor what their kids are watching and to take note of how long they're watching. Also, keeping television out of the bedroom means that kids' rooms are sanctuaries where they can study or read without distraction. In that vein, if you have young children, read to them. Children who are read to are more likely to do better in school and to read themselves. Besides, the time you spend reading together is the kind of quality time that watching television can never replace.

Watching television is still a good way to view movies as a family, keep up with breaking news, learn about nature's wonders, or laugh together at silly cartoons and sit-coms. But keep your household's viewing in check. TV should be just one among many entertainment outlets for your family.

- FIVE -

Have a Weekly Family Game Night

When was the last time you laughed so hard with your family that your sides hurt? Sure, talking to your children and having family meals together is important. But remembering to stop and play—and play and play!— with your kids is a must, too, no matter what their age.

Taking a night each week just to be silly together isn't just about the silliness. Regularly laughing and having fun together is one of the more reliable markers of a strong, well-adjusted family, experts say. And in this hyperfast and ultracompetitive world, teaching children that fun is an important part of life at *every* age is one of the best lessons you can give. Show them how important it is by making it a mandatory item on your family's weekly calendar.

Game night means no television and no serious discussions—except for serious strategizing against Dad and Sis, of course! Make your own house rules for each game you play, and teach your children the importance of winning and losing gracefully. Great games actively engage your kids' minds and are interactive tools that can help develop critical thinking, concentration, deductive reasoning, and math and spelling. That's certainly not something that can be said about hour upon hour of mind-numbing television shows or blast-'em-to-pieces video games.

Use game night as a chance to bask in accomplishments, to pass Go, to learn how to be a team player, and to revel in family. Just keep these "rules" in mind.

• Make sure everyone in the family gets a chance to regularly choose the game.

• Enshrine the winner's name on the refrigerator each week.

• Remember that losing just makes the next victory that much sweeter.

• Make sure you do as much laughing as you do game playing.

• Age isn't an excuse not to participate. If your children are teens, you can still have a night together; just change the games. Darts, billiards, foosball, Ping-Pong, or poker, anyone?

So go make a Jenga tower, build hotels on Boardwalk, beef up your vocabulary with Scrabble (*qwerty* will get you mega points on a double-word space; it's a real word, we swear!), fall down in Twister, say you're Sorry!, sink a battleship, put someone in check, and go see what Colonel Mustard is up to in the library! And for goodness sake, have a snack!

6

Monitor Computer Time

The Internet is one of the best educational tools children

can have. Where else can they check in on the pandas

with the National Zoo's Panda Cam, spend an hour

translating the number 1 song in France into English,

and then whiz over to Alaska to learn about glaciers?

The Internet makes our world smaller and more accessible by placing information about absolutely everything literally at our fingertips. But the Internet doesn't judge the quality or appropriateness of that information; as a parent, that's your job.

Unfortunately, the cyber world is full of criminals, bullies, pornography, hate, violence, and gossip. That's why keeping your kids safe online has to be a priority in your household. If you don't understand the Internet or are intimidated by computers and technology, it's time to learn how to use all of it. You can protect your children on the information highway only if *you* know how to navigate it as well.

Once you're relatively computer savvy, make sure you have Internet guidelines in place in your home. Here are some important rules for every child.

- Make sure your children know to never give out your address, phone number, last name, or any other pieces of information that could identify them or you. Check any pictures they want to post on the Web for identifiers as well.
- Never agree to face-to-face meetings with anyone originally met on the Internet—ever.
- Don't respond to any message that makes you feel uncomfortable. Make sure your kids tell you right away if any message they receive is mean or in any way untoward.
- Never download anything without parental permission.
- Don't share passwords with anyone except parents.
- No Web cams are allowed in the house—ever.
- Follow time limits jointly established for daily computer use.

Laying down rules is just one part of your duties. You should also tour the Internet with your children to get a sense of the sites they like to visit, the blogs they read, and the social networks they belong to. And make sure you talk about your children's Internet friends and activities just as you would any other friends or activities they have.

Finally, learn "cyberspeak" and "leetspeak." Knowing the lingo your children use online and in instant messages is an important way to decode what they're saying (such as POS, "parent over shoulder"). Check out NetLingo.com for a list of the cyber words a parent should know.

7

Write Two Wills

Nearly 75 percent of parents with minor children
do not have wills, according to a recent survey.
That's a shocking number.

Many people may think that wills are just for the wealthy, but the fact is, a will is the best way to ensure that your loved ones are properly taken care of. That's crucial for their peace of mind and yours. It's good for the country, too.

No matter how much money you have—or don't have—naming guardians for your children or recording your wishes about your medical care in a legal document can be crucial for your family if tragedy occurs.

Why? Let's say you have an agreement with your sister that she will take care of your children should anything happen to you. The problem is that without a will, a judge won't see your agreement as binding and could easily appoint someone else as guardian. What's more, in the absence of a will, family members can challenge a judge's ruling. If your brother thinks he should be your kids' guardian, he can fight your sister for custody. But that's not all. The money for this legal battle would come out of your estate, meaning that in essence, your children would pay for it.

Any good will should also include a property guardian, someone who can manage any money or property you leave to your children until they are old enough to take responsibility for it. This guardian can be the person who will raise your children, or it can be a financial adviser or someone else with financial savvy. Also, these days, you can leave specific instructions about how your money should be used, such as for a college fund. You can even leave detailed instructions about how your kids should be cared for, from the proper religious education to making sure they go to their favorite ice cream stand every summer.

Whether children are involved or not, everyone should create a separate *living will* as well. Incredible medical advances have made it possible to prolong the lives of the severely injured or ill indefinitely. Regardless of whether you think medical innovations are true lifesavers or artificial life extenders, your opinion won't matter unless it is formalized in a living will. Without this document, your life, or quality of life, could be subject to the opinion of a judge. It's up to you to ensure that your wishes are carried out. Besides, without a living will, your family may enter into a heartbreaking debate about what they think your true desires are. At least you can spare them that much—and possibly a court date, too.

- EIGHT -

Nurture Family Elders

Who are the elders in your family? The obvious answer is that they are your parents, grandparents, uncles, aunts, and eldest cousins—basically, any relative who's getting up in years. But that doesn't really answer the question, does it? In a well-grounded family, there is a big difference between being elderly and being an elder.

Elders are the storytellers, the cooks, the jokesters, the historians, the authorities, the knitters, the Scrabble champions, the raconteurs, the workhorses, the nurturers. They are the people we respect and turn to for answers and perspective, thanks to their many years of life. Most of all, they are the people who raised you and your loved ones and helped you grow into the people you are. For several decades, they carried the burden of caring for your family and leading it to better times. Now it's your turn to dote on them. Ensuring the welfare of our elders should come as naturally to us as raising our children.

Unfortunately, too many people take their parents' and grandparents' ability to care for themselves for granted. And in a country where so many of us live hundreds of miles from our families, looking after loved ones can be difficult to accomplish remotely. Even so, you should make sure your loved ones are taken care of no matter where they live, and try to look after any seniors living alone in your neighborhood, too. Taking responsibility for the venerable elders in our society is an imperative we all should heed. It's the mark of a decent, caring citizenry.

There are two parts to nurturing our elders. The one we focus on most is caring for their material needs—making sure they have safe homes, food to eat, and good doctors to tend to them. This is complicated and important stuff that requires serious effort—so much so that we often neglect the other aspect of caring for elders: tending to their hearts and souls. Here are some suggestions for the softer side of elder care.

• Treat every older person in your life with utter respect. Despite the toll age can take on health, appearance, and manner, inside every individual is a vibrant, powerful personality. Remember to love and laugh with the elderly without condescension—and without restraint!

• A component of respect is being tolerant of faults. Yes, they've told you the same story 183 times. Yes, their favorite pastime may seem to be gossip. Yes, they can be incessantly critical of you, the government, the weather, or the price of tomatoes. And yes, with love, patience, and cleverness, you can change the subject and bring out the best in them.

• Alone or with your children, take your parents', grandparents', or elderly neighbors' oral history. Each person has a story, and older generations have faced challenges most of us have never had to consider, from drastic changes in the social climate of America to immigration stories and hard-won successes. Take the time to get to know the elders in your life as citizens of the world.

• Include them in your life whenever you can. Sending a funny e-mail to friends? Add seniors' e-addresses to the list. Having a picnic? Invite them along. Yes, it may mean more work for you, but remember all the times they did extra work to accommodate you when you were a child?

• Acknowledge their fears and frailties and when you can, step in to assist. For example, be their spokesperson when the health-care system proves too tough for them to navigate, or gently offer to help manage their financial affairs when it becomes clear they are struggling to make good choices.

• Subscribe to the AARP magazine at AARPmagazine.org. It's filled with great articles and tips about helping loved ones navigate their later years with confidence and knowledge.

Sharing
Yourself

If everyone in America volunteered for just 1 hour a week, the face of our nation would change. Troubled individuals would be cared for. Polluted spaces would be cleaned up. Disadvantaged children would be mentored. Adults without the support, education, or skills to escape poverty would get the helping hand they need.

Too often, we think it requires a large-scale program to make large-scale improvements. It doesn't. It just takes caring people. Sure, writing checks to charities is a wonderful thing, and Americans are very generous that way. But to truly help people, nothing is more potent than sharing your time and skills.

Volunteering isn't just about giving, though. The grand secret of volunteering is that you gain as much as you give. In a country saturated with cults of celebrity, wild consumerism, and an extreme focus on appearances, a little volunteer work can be soul changing. Volunteering—even for only an hour a week—reminds you that greatness comes from quiet integrity found within yourself, not from financial achievement or a killer wardrobe. When you contribute to other people's lives in a meaningful way, you define your own success. By sharing, you can change the world. Now that's a value we Americans should all embrace.

Set a Monthly Volunteer Quota

It is a sad truth that millions of people in America need help. For each needy person, though, there are many people who have stable, secure lives. Imagine the potential of our nation if, for every person in need, one or more volunteers came forward to help.

We could keep kids who live in rough neighborhoods off the streets; we could ensure that no elderly people find themselves alone in the world; we could make sure that in a nation with so much, no child goes to bed hungry; we could prepare more students for jobs or college; and we could help struggling families face life with confidence and integrity.

Contributing a few hours a month to volunteering is a mandate we should all follow. The trouble is, most of us are busy—very busy. That means that if we don't schedule time and make arrangements for volunteering in advance, it probably won't happen. The answer: set a monthly quota—just 1 to

4 hours—and plan to fulfill it. This small investment in your community could literally change the course of someone's life for the better.

Better yet, make volunteering a regular family activity. Use the opportunity to teach your children about charity, about giving, and about the responsibility all of us have for each other. It is said that of those to whom much is given, much is expected. We can argue about the politics of the day (and we should!), but in America, we receive much more than most other people on the planet. Our homes; our education; our abundant food, water, and natural resources—we are given much. So expect much of yourselves.

Offer up your professional skills, your hard labor, or your kindness—it doesn't matter. Whether you coach basketball after work, or read to children on your lunch hour, or spend an occasional evening keeping seniors company, any time spent and any contribution offered is worthwhile. Just be sure that however you choose to serve, you commit to it fully.

• DoSomething.org is a great site for young people to find out how they can volunteer. Devoted entirely to youth volunteerism, Do Something has great ideas and opportunities that can really inspire the younger set.

• At VolunteerMatch.org, you can enter your zip code or interests and find a volunteer opportunity that best fits your lifestyle. With a database of thousands of opportunities, it's a great place to get started or to look for out-of-the-box ideas that could work for you.

• At HelpYourCommunity.org, you can find tips on how you can help children in need in your own community. Look at the list of "101 Things You Can Do" to be a positive influence on kids and think about how you might make a difference.

• Many workplaces now offer volunteer partnerships. See if yours is linked to any groups; you may discover that taking an hour off a week from work to volunteer at a soup kitchen is allowed or even encouraged. Many workplaces also donate money to the organization you volunteer with if you submit proof of regular activity.

• If you attend a church, synagogue, mosque, or other house of worship, there's bound to be a raft of volunteer opportunities available there. Many of the most devoted volunteers in the country come from spiritual centers.

- TEN -

Have a Charity Plan

Americans donated nearly $250 billion to charities
and nonprofit organizations in 2005, according to
CharityNavigator.com. That's roughly $850 from
every man, woman, and child in our country. Without
question, we are a generous nation.

We do this without hesitation and with no recognition of our
good deeds. Americans contribute because it's the right thing
to do, because our fellow citizens are in need.

Yet often, we act spontaneously. The vast majority of givers
make donations based on letters in the mail or solicitations on
the phone. We often don't know the amount of our cumulative
donations, how our money will be spent, or whether our chosen charities are known for spending their money wisely.
Sometimes giving in a moment of sheer altruism may also
mean giving blindly. So this year, create a charity plan.
Here's how.

- Start each year by creating a charity budget based on what you think is a reasonable amount for you and your family to donate over the coming 12 months.

- Next, think about what causes are most meaningful to you. Finding a cure for diseases that have touched your loved ones? Feeding the poor overseas? Helping local parks? Supporting your alma mater? Come up with a reasonable division among the charities you wish to support.

- With that done, you can be both selective and proactive in targeting your donations. Doing research is easy at CharityNavigator.org, where you can search more than 5,000 charities to find objective information on their spending habits and effectiveness. The site will provide charts that break down expenses and revenue as well as give an overall score and rating. You can find similar services at Give.org, an extension of the Better Business Bureau, where a thorough report is issued on each charity and nonprofit. Both sites are easy to read and navigate, and the information they provide is often eye-opening.

- Do not give cash. If you hand cash to a stranger, there's no way to ensure that your donation will reach the charity. Instead, write a check—made out to the organization, not the person collecting the funds. That way, you'll also have a record of your donation for tax purposes.

- Do not donate to a solicitor who e-mails you. Today, charity scams are rampant. It's very easy to mimic the logo and style of an official charity in an e-mail or on a Web site. And be skeptical of charities whose names sound familiar yet not quite right. Many scam artists slightly alter the name of a well-known charity to trade on the real organization's good reputation. If you do donate online, check the Web addresses and names against those listed on CharityNavigator.org or Give.org.

• Do not feel pressured to give to a solicitor who stops you on the street. The charity will be just as delighted to receive your contribution the next day, after you've gone home and researched their organization.

• Just because an organization is "tax exempt" doesn't mean that your contribution is tax deductible. Make sure the charity you are donating to considers donations tax deductible and that you can get a receipt.

This year, give smart. When you know the integrity of a charity is beyond reproach, you just may consider giving even more.

- ELEVEN -

Be an Off-Season Donation Hero

In the days after September 11, 2001, thousands of people lined up to donate blood. After Hurricane Katrina's wrath, the country responded with unprecedented donations of food and water.

And every year during the holidays, families turn up at soup kitchens with canned goods and toys.

America has a great heart, but sometimes it takes a crisis or a holiday to remind us of those in need. And during a crisis, the person who donated blood a week earlier, regularly gives food and water to the Red Cross, or dropped off supplies at soup kitchens in March or August is often the unsung, quiet hero who makes the greatest impact. After all, the first bottles of water to reach hurricane victims are the ones that are already waiting, ready to go, on the shelves of charities before storms hit—not the ones that come later, once the nation sees the aftermath on television.

Charities, nonprofits, and churches that look after the home-less, the elderly, or families in need accept donations year-round. But don't think of just canned food. Most groups that help the needy are looking for all of the essentials that most of us take for granted, so make a "souped-up shoebox": Every time you buy a new pair of shoes, also buy a toothbrush, deodorant, soap, lotion, and a comb. Throw the toiletries into the shoebox and take it to your local church, shelter, or Red Cross center. Your new shoes may just help someone else put their best foot forward!

Let giving be a year long endeavor. If you're a healthy adult, donate blood every other month—that's just six times a year. Making sure there is a safe, sustained blood supply for our sol-diers, for victims of natural disasters, for people who have traumatic accidents, and for the sick is an amazing way to honor your community and your country. Giving blood is easy, personal, and just may save a life the very day you donate. Check out GiveLife.org to find out where you can donate blood.

Think about giving as a normal part of your life—from every new pair of sneakers or stilettos to a pint of life for someone who hurts. Buy that extra toy at Christmastime to make a child's season a little brighter, but this year, buy one in June as well. You may just remind a child in need that birthdays are special, too.

12
- TWELVE -

Adopt a Soldier

We all support our troops and care about their safety and well-being, but did you know that there's something more you can do to raise a soldier's spirits? Adopting a soldier, or even a whole platoon, can affect the mood of the troops and even have reverberations around the world.

Unfortunately, not every soldier has the love and support of a strong family, and all soldiers struggle with homesickness and reduced morale during long deployments in foreign lands. That's why writing cards to soldiers, shipping blankets and socks, and sending DVDs and novels can be so important and meaningful to our young people in dangerous war zones.

The founder of SoldiersAngels.org is the mother of a soldier who was stationed in Iraq in 2003. She was concerned when her son told her that some of his fellow troops weren't receiving mail. Today, SoldiersAngels.org can arrange for people to become "angels" by sending cards and care packages to soldiers each month—including wounded soldiers who need hope and cheer to come home healthy. At the site, you can also make a donation toward Kevlar blankets to help protect the troops by clicking on the "Armor Up" button.

At AdoptAPlatoon.org, individuals, couples, families, youth groups, and schoolchildren can adopt a soldier or even an entire platoon. In addition to letters and care packages, the site offers other unique ways to give, such as donating crayons to help the youngest victims of war, a summertime bug spray and sunscreen drive, and a project to create bright, fun pillowcases for injured soldiers.

Our soldiers are not just our sisters, brothers, husbands, daughters, fathers, and best friends; they are the face of America. While fighting terrorism abroad, our troops also meet the thousands of innocent people in war-torn countries. They high-five the children, hug mourning grandmothers, and help rebuild infrastructures. Supporting our troops is not just about morale; it's about goodwill the world over.

- THIRTEEN -

Make Martin Luther King Day
a Day of Service

The Rev. Dr. Martin Luther King Jr. believed that
any individual has the power to become anything he
sets his mind to. He taught us to create success
under any circumstances.

Dr. King's messages of tolerance, equality, and active citizenship deeply touched Americans and many other people all over the world. Today, his legacy lives on in the noble mandate of the organizers of Martin Luther King Day: "Live up to the purpose and potential of America by uniting and taking action to make this country a better place to live."

Since MLK Day is a national holiday, most Americans have the day off—no school, no work, no pressing responsibilities. But this year, instead of using the day as the last leg of a casual three-day weekend, make Dr. King's holiday a "day on." For years, the King Day of Service has honored Dr. King's teachings by encouraging people everywhere to devote the day to community service. By bringing people of all faiths and races together to work on large projects, such as repainting a home for the elderly or building a school playground, the spirit of selflessness and charity embodied by Dr. King are brought to life.

At MLKDay.gov, you can find a state-by-state list of projects planned for Martin Luther King Day in your area. You can also find resources to help you organize your own community project, and you can download an MLK Day Toolkit with tips for putting together any kind of service project. If MLK Day isn't considered a work holiday where you live, arrange to do a project on Labor Day or Groundhog Day or any other day that's convenient for you.

Be sure to involve your children or the child you mentor. Use the day as an opportunity to teach the next generation about equality for all people and about the spirit of our country. Paint a mural, landscape a public park, hold a legal clinic, or renovate a church—use your skills to help keep Dr. King's dream alive and to continue to fulfill America's promise.

- FOURTEEN -

Be a Mentor

As adults, we often have more skills than we realize.

Is it a coincidence that kids require skills they

often don't realize exist?

Take the children of parents who never went to college. How can they effectively navigate the admissions and financial aid process without wise help? Or think of children growing up with inner-city violence and despair. How can they rise out of their situation without being shown a better path and a reason to take it?

One-on-one mentoring remains one of the best ways to help direct children in challenging situations toward a better future. If you are already raising children or have a busy career, it may seem as if there's just no time in your life to add another responsibility, but almost all mentoring programs are flexible about fitting meeting times into a busy schedule. And once you establish trust, meeting times become a more natural part of your regular routine. Who knows? The child you mentor may just grow up to change the world.

There are many wonderful ways to mentor. Ask yourself if you have any particular skills or knowledge that might be useful to a young person. Perhaps you can take on an apprentice in your small business or teach junior achievement at a local elementary school. For many potential mentors, just approaching a local school or community religious outlet is enough to find a great way to help out; often these schools and organizations either already have mentoring programs in place or work with associations that do.

Another place to begin is at Mentoring.org. At this terrific Web site, you can enter your zip code to find a raft of mentoring opportunities near you, then decide on a program that works best with your busy schedule. Of course, there are a number of reputable programs throughout the country that you can contact as well. The following are some amazing national programs that recognize how important it is that every child be given a fair shot at success.

• The Boys and Girls Clubs of America (BGCA.org) provides after-school activities and leadership training for kids in at-risk neighborhoods.

• The Experience Corps (ExperienceCorps.org) specializes in matching mentors over 55 with young people.

• Big Brothers Big Sisters of America (BBBSA.org) arranges one-on-one relationships between kids and mentors.

- FIFTEEN -

Adopt a Pet

Dogs and cats are playful and cute and mischievous and loyal and happy and nonjudgmental and generally the best friends anyone could ever have. It's no wonder that statistically, people who have pets are happier and live longer than people without them.

After all, how upset can you be after a tough day when a Labrador mix with a heart of gold is positively over the moon with joy that you are home?

If you're ready for a first pet or want to add another to your family, please consider adopting a shelter animal who needs a forever home. These days, people are quick to buy those cute pets they see in store windows, but unfortunately, impulsive purchases ultimately mean more needy animals on the streets or in shelters. According to the Humane Society of the United States (HSUS), 3 to 4 million abandoned and stray cats and dogs are euthanized in shelters each year.

Statistics haven't been gathered on the subject, but given that there are thousands of government-run animal shelters across the country, it's likely that billions of our tax dollars are spent each year to deal with the problem of homeless pets. Think about it: Do we really want to spend so much government cash solving problems caused mostly by failed pet owners?

Perhaps we can remedy this situation individually. Americans are more than happy to shell out billions of dollars for designer pet clothes and accessories—a trend that continues to grow—so we clearly love our animals. Perhaps it's time to be a bit more charitable to homeless pets.

Most shelters have great programs that allow you to get to know an animal or animals before making a firm commitment. Take a dog home for a night before adopting him. You may find that the one you're considering is too much to handle—or you may fall head over heels! Also, if you're mad for a specific breed, you should know that 25 percent of the animals in shelters are purebred.

If you decide to adopt, find out if the animal you've chosen is spayed or neutered. If not, or if it's a puppy or kitten, commit to having the surgery done. If cost is a factor, many shelters can give you information on low-cost programs. Population control is still the best way to keep animals off the streets and in loving homes. Go to ASPCA.org or HSUS.org for more information on needy pets in your area.

- SIXTEEN -

Donate Your Old Books

Great stories never lose their value. While that tattered, dusty thriller on your shelf may not look like much, the story inside it is just as adventurous and exciting as it was the day you first bought it—especially to someone who hasn't read it yet.

These days, old books have a second chance of being read and enjoyed anew, thanks to a host of organizations that can turn your used books into charity dollars. Instead of tossing your old textbooks in the basement or jumping on Ebay.com every time you finish a novel, why not donate your books to a great cause? It's tax deductible, and you don't have to lift a finger. Nowadays, many book charities will come right to your house and pick up everything from old children's books to the cookbooks you forgot were in the cupboard!

At GotBooks.com, you can donate your books either by sending them in or by scheduling a pickup right at your doorstep.

Got Books organizes huge book sales with profits directed toward several charities, such as Dollars for Scholars, a higher-education fund; children's sports associations such as Pop Warner Football and the Babe Ruth League; and Books for Soldiers, a group that gets book "want lists" from troops stationed overseas and delivers the books to the soldiers. GotBooks.com will also pick up your old videos, DVDs, and CDs, so think about doing some spring cleaning a little early this year.

Of course, there are lots of other great places to donate used books. One example is the Used Books Café in New York City. There, 100 percent of the profits from book sales go to The Housing Works, a nonprofit group that provides housing, health care, and other services to people living with HIV and AIDS. And you don't have to live anywhere near New York to help: You can mail in your donation, and they will make sure that you receive a receipt for a tax deduction. Go to HousingWorks.org for more information.

Then there's FirstBook.org, a charity dedicated to putting books in the hands of low-income children. First Book has been instrumental in ensuring that the youngest victims of Hurricane Katrina can escape into the magic of a great tale. To donate, check out FirstBook.org for more information or go to TheLiteracySite.com for more ways to help.

If you want to stay local, most churches and pubic libraries are great places to start. So give your books a shelf life that really makes a difference—it's a happy ending for everyone.

- SEVENTEEN -

Coach a Team

Each of us has abilities, whether physical, mental, or social. What most of us don't realize is that teaching these skills to children can help transform their lives.

That's why coaching can have such an enormous impact. For America's kids, learning not only a skill but also how to work together is the perfect foundation for their future success.

Maybe you don't like athletics or haven't pursued them since grade school, but don't give up on coaching just yet. Neither coaching nor teamwork is the exclusive province of sports. The stunning resurgence in the popularity of spelling bees demonstrates that competition, dedication, and big goals can be part of all children's lives. In fact, there are all kinds of coaching experiences available that have nothing to do with muscles and games. From debating to building robots to making music, team-oriented programs for kids are exploding, and they all need people like us to help.

Think about your skills. Are you good at chess? Tennis? Maybe you orate like Daniel Webster. Then find out what programs are at your local schools, library, or community center that align with your specialty. And if there isn't a program, take the next step. For children in areas in which funds are scarce, there aren't many activities to choose from at schools or community centers. Stand up for those kids and ask yourself what you can do to create a new "team" opportunity.

Remember also that children who are new to a craft or sport don't need a guru, just some guidance. In other words, you don't have to be Tiger Woods to teach golf or Annie Leibowitz to teach photography. You just have to be willing to share yourself. Show a child how to play Scrabble, solve crossword puzzles, debate, care for bonsai, build Lego sculptures, work with papier-mâché, or figure out Rubik's cube. There's a tournament out there for just about every skill; why not give a child the thrill of being recognized for a new talent? And yes, coaching baseball, football, basketball, soccer, or any other traditional sport is always an amazing way to give.

We can't emphasize it enough: Our society's obsession with popular culture and video games is often in direct conflict with the values of hard work and collaboration, and ongoing improvement that we so want our children to have. Absent a counterbalance, these cultural forces teach kids to become passive spectators in life. Help children learn that they can achieve anything they set their minds on—and not watch life go by from the lonely isolation of a sofa.

- EIGHTEEN -

Practice Random Acts of Kindness

You've probably heard the expression, "Practice random kindness and senseless acts of beauty," but have you ever actually done it?

Have you ever paid for the next five cars at a tollbooth or handed fresh flowers to the woman who sells you the paper every morning? These may seem like silly things to do, but when you show someone a kindness, you change the way that person feels for the rest of the day. And that often changes how *you* feel, too.

Each of has an astonishing amount of power; we can alter the course of someone's day—even that of a stranger, whom we may never see again—with a simple gesture of kindness. And our act may inspire that person to bestow a kindness on someone else. Who knows? You just may start a ripple effect of kindness that continues for weeks to come.

Joy is a potent gift to spread around. Imagine if everyone were in a good mood at once. Easier still, imagine if *you* were the recipient of surprising kindness. You might laugh at that guy who cuts you off in traffic instead of honking and yelling and putting him and yourself in a terrible mood before heading home to your family. You might forgive the woman who made you the wrong sandwich because, well, mistakes happen. Maybe you'll even get a free sandwich rather than the defensive attitude she might have given you if you had made her feel bad.

Here are some great ways to practice random acts of kindness.

- Bring bagels, cookies, or fresh strawberries to your coworkers.
- Write to the boss of someone who helped you and praise that employee.
- Put fun notes in your kids' lunches.
- Offer free car washes to your neighbors.
- Pass out free sodas to city workers as they haul your garbage away one morning or fix the telephone wires on your street.
- Offer to baby-sit for free for your favorite couple.
- Let your staff leave an hour early.
- The next time you have extra tickets for a game, give them to your bus driver or favorite janitor.
- Leave a big tip for a harried waiter.
- Pay for the meal of the person behind you at a drive-through restaurant.
- Invite someone new over for dinner.
- Buy cold drinks for everyone in your row at the ballpark.
- Offer a surprise thank-you gift to people who routinely provide service—the security guard at work, the waitress who

always serves you with a smile, the teacher who takes extra care of your child.

- Make sending thank-you cards part of your life. Write to former mentors, teachers, friends, or anyone who once was kind to you or to whom you just want to express your love.
- Clean up. Picking up litter as you see it keeps your town beautiful and may inspire your friends to notice litter more often as they walk around, too.
- Give compliments openly and freely—sometimes even to strangers. It's not inappropriate, for example, to tell a parent at a restaurant or store that you've been impressed by how wonderfully their children are behaving and that they should be very proud.

For more great ideas and inspiration, visit the Random Acts of Kindness Foundation online at ActsofKindness.org. The foundation can get you started practicing kindness with classroom kits for teachers, community guides, kindness clubs, kindness Web pages, a kindness newsletter, free kindness e-cards, and a raft of kindness events. Find out how other people are being kind and pay it forward.

Improving
Communities

What is it about small-town living—picket fences, general stores, friendly neighbors—that Americans are so drawn to? That's easy to answer: It's the sense of community. We have an innate desire for that one place where everyone really does know your name, where you look out for one another, and where you share a sense of pride in the patch of Earth you share with one another. What we sometimes forget, though, is that communities come in all shapes and sizes. An apartment building in downtown Chicago is a community; so is a suburban tract in Houston, a swath of row houses in Boston, or a retirement complex in Tampa. Communities are the building blocks of America, and that's why they are so important.

America is an awfully large and overwhelming place, but in a community, there is common identity, kinship, and cooperation. The success of our country is wholly dependent on the success of our communities. Without people on the ground making connections, helping one another, looking out for one another, and just making friends, our society lacks meaning. Communities and neighborhoods are the true first responders in the event of a natural disaster or just a baby-sitting emergency. Caring for your community is a fantastic way to care for the country.

NINETEEN

Map Your Neighborhood

Remember when kids used to just go out and play, and grownups spent evenings sharing stories on the front porch? When the outdoors didn't compete with video games, and "stranger danger" wasn't such a grave concern for parents?

At some point, we all seemed to decide that letting children tear down the street on a dirt bike without a helmet didn't seem like such a good idea anymore. That's smart. But we also started to lock the gate and move our fun from the front yard to the backyard (or the TV room). We stopped meeting our neighbors; we became less friendly and more suspicious.

There's nothing more important than protecting your family, but isolation doesn't equal protection. Connecting with your neighbors not only lets you know the personalities that surround you, it also provides you with surprisingly positive and helpful resources in times of need.

So here's your task: Make a map of your neighborhood (or better yet, print one out! GoogleMaps can provide an aerial photo of most U.S. neighborhoods and all the houses in it) and "fill it out." Can you write down the names of the occupants of every household, including children, pets, and parents? See how many you can do, and then take a walk through the neighborhood and meet people. Find out who has children at the same school as yours or which homes have adults who stay at home all day. Learn who is friendliest and who is lonely and in need of a neighborly hand. You may even discover who has a magic touch at gardening, or a great movie or music collection, or the best "crisis" kitchen (just in case you need a cup of sugar, a splash of olive oil, or a mug of freshly imported dark-roast Costa Rican coffee).

If you live in an apartment, do exactly the same. Learn with whom you share a floor or a building. Have a casual mixer or just go door to door and introduce yourself with a smile and a handshake. Sharing the true reason for your visit—that you feel it's important to meet your neighbors and want them to know you as well—should quell any suspicions.

Whether you live in an urban high-rise, or a suburban tract, or on a rural lane, chances are your neighbors will be thrilled by your friendliness. Perhaps a few dinners will come out of it. Perhaps you'll find a baby-sitter or a way to help a neighbor who is in need. And a year or two later, you may just find that your neighborhood has become a friendlier, more caring place.

20

Start a Neighborhood Watch

Crime prevention is one of the chief goals of any caring
neighborhood. Living in a low-crime neighborhood
means your children can ride their bikes down the street
or play hide-and-seek in the yard. It means soaring
property values and restful nights.

Put simply, a safe neighborhood—and the freedom it grants
you to live exactly as you wish, without fear—is one of the
best parts of the American dream.

So how do you prevent crime? Start by participating in a
Neighborhood Watch program. Statistics show that these programs remain one of the most successful and effective ways of
achieving the safety and security you desire.

You and your neighbors know better than any police officer if
someone is out of place in your neighborhood or loitering on the
corner every Friday night. When cooperation between neighborhood groups and the police or sheriff's department is established

and neighbors report suspicious activity, statistics show that crime can decrease dramatically. Joining a Neighborhood Watch program will mean getting the tools and training to keep your street safe. A good program should include:

- Home security inspections by crime prevention officers
- Upgrading locks and outdoor lighting and even installing alarms
- Asking neighbors to watch for suspicious activity when a house is empty
- Marking valuable property with an identifying number to discourage theft and help law enforcement agencies identify and return stolen property
- Organizing block parents and block groups to assist children and the elderly if they appear to be distressed, in danger, or lost
- Meeting in neighborhood groups with crime prevention officers to discuss needs and strategies
- Developing neighborhood telephone trees to quickly alert each other about criminal activity in the area
- Encouraging the development of signals for use in adjacent homes when someone needs help
- Identifying the neighborhood's participation in the program with decals and signs

Because no one knows your street better than you do, taking the initiative to work with authorities through a Neighborhood Watch program can maximize law enforcement. To get started, visit USAOnWatch.org. For street decals and signs, visit Neighborhood Watch online at NNWI.org.

- TWENTY-ONE -

Go Downtown

Shortly after World War II, America's downtowns began a long, slow descent into decay. The main reason: suburbs.

As more people moved out of cities in pursuit of bigger yards and easier living, many of our downtowns started to resemble ghost towns—shadow cities where some people worked but too few lived, places that felt empty on weekends and a little scary after dark.

The impact of this shift was deeper than many people realize. Mostly, we think in terms of economic impact—how the decline in population has hurt cities' tax bases, leaving many impoverished and driving businesses away. But there's a more individual impact as well. Urban centers are unique, filled with great architecture, quirky boutiques, joyous festivals, classic theaters, sidewalk cafés, and other delights that are absent from contemporary shopping malls and suburban thoroughfares.

But a rebound is occurring. Cities around the country are seeing major revitalization efforts aimed at creating downtowns that people will flock to. From small Florida towns and Midwestern hubs such as Cincinnati and Milwaukee to coastal cities dotting the Pacific Northwest, city museums, old theaters, and weathered storefronts are getting facelifts. Suddenly, microbreweries, art galleries, loft apartments, and street performances are flourishing in old factory buildings, armories, row houses, and town squares.

There's the famous Dinosaur Bar-B-Que in Syracuse, New York; ghost tours in Lexington, Virginia; incredible antique shopping in Galena, Illinois; and some of the best art in the country in Santa Fe, New Mexico. What special attractions does your city offer? Great American downtowns are excellent places to check out local artists and shop owners and discover unique gifts and culture. Mostly, though, downtowns are places to run into your friends, neighbors, and family as you browse store windows or sip coffee at a local café. Downtowns are where the great musicians come to play, where the theater comes alive, and where nightlife means more than just a movie at the local multiplex.

So whether you live in the suburbs, the exurbs, or right in the city, make a point of heading downtown. Take a long walk, visit a museum and a gallery, do some window shopping, have a great meal, and catch a show. Supporting America's downtowns keeps our sense of local culture and color alive and keeps our cities' economies vibrant.

- TWENTY-TWO -

Join the PTA

If you have children or are a teacher, join the PTA.
As the nation's largest child-advocacy association,
the Parent Teacher Association is a stalwart for
excellence in schools and is an important national
proponent of quality education for all children.

But what makes the PTA truly special is its effectiveness at individual schools. Your local PTA supports and protects critical programs such as art and music classes. It raises funds for programs the school district can't afford. And it provides ways for parents to get involved in their children's education far more effectively.

By joining your neighborhood PTA chapter, you automatically become a member of the state and national associations. At these higher levels, the PTA supports a raft of activities designed to put education at the top of every family's to-do list, such as the PTA Goes to Work Program, which partners with the

Department of Labor to provide job training and career information; the Parent Involvement Schools of Excellence Certification, which is aimed at increasing parent involvement in local schools; back-to-school programs and after-school programs; Reflections, an arts program; and workshops and seminars about topics such as health, nutrition, and bullying.

But it's often at the local level that parents experience the greatest benefits of PTA involvement. Active members get into the schools, create programs for kids, assist teachers, talk regularly with principals, and become part of the school community. And when your children see you at their school helping and participating, imagine the positive message they receive!

In return, joining the PTA grants you access to tons of resources and benefits, including:

• An annual reference manual with tips on using the PTA effectively and information on the latest education issues.

• The official magazine of the PTA, *Our Children*, with articles about parenting, health, and, of course, education.

• The Member-to-Member Network, a program that can connect PTA members to members of Congress for help with legislative issues affecting your PTA group.

• Online parenting resources and newsletters.

With services such as these, it should come as no surprise that most members of Congress have at one time been or are now standing members of the PTA. In fact, the PTA has a wonderful reputation for being the training ground for future community leaders. So join now and give your child a voice, too.

TWENTY-THREE

Learn a Lifesaving Technique

Did you know that up to 80 percent of all out-of-hospital cardiac arrests happen at home? If a member of your family went into cardiac arrest, would you know what to do? Being trained in cardiopulmonary resuscitation, or CPR, can mean the difference between life and death for someone you know.

Right now, a staggering 95 percent of sudden cardiac arrest victims die before they even make it to a hospital, but a bystander with CPR training can *double* someone's chance of survival. If everyone in your household took an afternoon to learn CPR, the chances of someone in your family dying of cardiac arrest would drop dramatically. Arming yourself with the ability to do CPR means that you may just find yourself on the frontier of reducing the number of preventable deaths in America. Imagine having the power to sustain a life until paramedics can arrive!

Learning CPR is simple. Go to the American Heart Association (AHA) Web site, AmericanHeart.org, to find a CPR class near you. Or you can arrange for AHA instructors to come to your workplace for a CPR demonstration—a great option if getting away from work during the day is challenging. The more people around you who know CPR, the better! If you don't find a convenient local course, you can even train in your home with the AHA's Family and Friends CPR Anytime kit. This training program takes just 22 minutes and comes complete with a practice mannequin, a training DVD, and a CPR booklet. For less than $30, everyone in your house (invite the neighbors, too!) can get training in this essential lifesaving skill.

Most CPR courses also cover the Heimlich maneuver, but if not, make sure you have this vital skill under your belt as well. For quick instruction in the Heimlich maneuver, go to HeimlichInstitute.org for easy illustrated techniques. Be sure to bookmark the Web page for a quick refresher anytime.

One day, you may be the first responder in a life-or-death situation. If you have the right skills, you can keep someone alive until an ambulance arrives. Take 22 minutes and empower yourself with the knowledge needed to save a life.

24
- TWENTY-FOUR -

Support Your Local Orchestra

There are few things that can bring joy to almost every person on the planet, yet that is the power of a live orchestra performance.

For nearly everyone, from a poverty-stricken child in Memphis to an elderly millionaire in Miami, spending a few hours at a symphony hall stops time, erases the day's struggles, and replenishes the soul.

Think about it. What child doesn't remember the majesty of their first class trip to hear an orchestra? At the other end of the scale, what better ambassadors are there for the American people than our great orchestras, performing to rave reviews in capitals around the world?

Yet orchestras in America are struggling. With arts education programs dwindling in public schools, and with so many forms of popular music and media vying for our attention, it's no surprise that attending a symphony performance isn't a high priority for most Americans.

That doesn't mean we're not interested, though. According to the National Endowment for the Arts, tens of millions of Americans enjoy classical music—yet only a fraction of that number go to concerts. It's time to change that.

Most cities in the country have their own symphony orchestras, and many orchestra associations are active in arts education in schools and in teaching children about classical music and how to select instruments for themselves. This is an amazing gift. Did you know that children who play an instrument do better in math and science and that they even score at least 50 points higher than the national average on standardized tests such as the SAT? But this is just part of why supporting your local orchestra is tantamount to supporting the very fabric of your community.

There is nothing quite like feeling surrounded by music, watching the musicians' intensity, or just closing your eyes and feeling the rhythm of percussion, or the quiet poignancy of a string note. Take your family to an outdoor performance and enjoy a picnic, make the symphony your best first date, invite friends who have never been to an orchestra performance to join you, and make the symphony a must for the Fourth of July and Christmas. Here are some other ideas.

• Go to MeetTheMusic.org to find a great symphony orchestra near you and to learn more about enjoying classical music.

• Check out the American Symphony Orchestra League's Web site at Symphony.org to find out more about how you can help keep local symphonies playing strong for years to come.

- TWENTY-FIVE -

Take a Public Speaking Course

Earning success in a competitive world takes more than just a good résumé. Out in the real world, good ideas are often only as good as the person presenting them. Learning people skills and the art of communicating clearly, dynamically, and persuasively is a potent way to ensure your own success—and to fully participate in your community.

By taking a public speaking course, you can master the skills required in the current American landscape. Today, with a 24-hour news cycle, hundreds of television stations, and massive amounts of information on the Internet, the need to be able to speak clearly and effectively is greater than ever. Doctors are interviewed on the local news during flu season, lawyers are asked to discuss the big cases of the day, business leaders comment on the region's economy, and just about anyone can be asked to do a man-on-the-street interview. These days, if you have interesting ideas or a specific type of expertise, chances are you're going to have to speak about it in a very public way.

Even in the private world in which most of our careers take place, public speaking skills are vital to our success. Making a proposal to a superior, teaching a classroom full of bored children, pitching an idea to an organization, or acquitting yourself well at an important social function are all situations in which we daily experience the need to express clear, organized thoughts that will help create serious interest in our ideas and opinions. A public speaking course can help you identify how to be assertive without being aggressive, how to read your audience, how to control a conversation or interview while maintaining a pleasant demeanor, how to think on your feet, and how to deal with tricky or difficult responses and questions.

Even if you never attend a board meeting or find yourself on television, you may be asked to make a toast, give a eulogy, host a dinner party, or just voice your opinion at a town meeting. Why not do so with confidence? Great ideas have made our country unique and inventive. Continue the tradition with public speaking skills for a modern world. Check out Toastmasters International for quick tips and ideas on public speaking at Toastmasters.org/tips.asp.

Build a 72-Hour Emergency Kit

The nationwide lessons of the new millennium have
been severe. We've faced the worst terrorist attack
ever on our country's soil. We've seen wave after
wave of weather-related tragedies. And we've learned
of grave new health risks, such as bird flu, SARS,
and mad cow disease.

What's more, we've witnessed the bitter aftermath of crises,
particularly the slow evacuations, the lack of supplies, and the
challenges of staging a comprehensive response.

There is much people can say about this unusual string of
misfortunes, but there is one lesson all of us must learn from
it: While we can't always predict a crisis, we sure can do better
to prepare for it.

The Department of Homeland Security recommends that
every family have a three-day emergency supply kit. The idea

is that it should take first responders no more than three days to reach you, so everyone should be prepared to survive on their own for 72 hours. At the Department of Homeland Security's preparedness Web site, Ready.gov, you can find lots of ideas about how to prepare for emergencies. A basic kit should include:

- Water: 3 gallons per person
- Food: at least a three-day supply of nonperishables
- Can opener
- Battery-powered radio and extra batteries
- Waterproof matches
- Utility knife
- Flashlight and extra batteries
- First-aid kit
- Whistle to signal for help
- Dust mask to help filter contaminated air, and plastic sheeting and duct tape to protect a room from contaminated air
- Moist towelettes, garbage bags, and plastic ties
- Essential medications

If you're anxious about making your own kit or about forgetting a crucial item, there are many great emergency kits on the market today, many of which use lightweight materials. GetReadyGear.com, EmergencyEssentials.com, LifeSecure.com, Nitro-Pak.com, and AlwaysBePrepared.com all have complete emergency kits and the supplies to put together your own. Be sure to tailor your emergency kit to your own needs.

- TWENTY-SEVEN -

Get a Library Card

We live in a nation in which no matter what town you are in, you can walk into the local library, sit down, and read. In your own community, you can leave with a book with no more effort than it takes to apply for a library card. How great is that?

Our libraries and librarians offer a rich world of literature, information, media, and fun. The local librarian can be your research assistant for a term paper, a historian, a genealogist, and a guide all at once. And libraries are often the best repositories of local history, centers for adult literacy, and locations for story hours and poetry readings. Supporting a library is a prime way to support your community and promote the kinds of values we all espouse. What better way to say, "I support reading, education, and learning" than through a commitment to your local library?

There are lots of ways to get involved, but none is more seminal than obtaining a library card. That little card is an all-access pass that allows you to borrow books, movies, and music; attend special events; and enjoy a sanctuary for undisturbed reading. Introduce your children to the library with their first card—their very own passport to the magical world of books. This wonderful privilege makes children feel special and inspires them to delve into reading and choosing their own books. Besides, with a library card in your pocket, you may just be inspired to read more yourself—a superb way to model learning!

To find out more about libraries and all they have to offer, go to Library Lovers at LibrarySupport.net (www.library support.net/librarylovers/how.html). There you can find out what libraries around the country are doing and learn more about what you can do to show your support and appreciation for the library in your community.

- TWENTY-EIGHT -

Get Your Company Involved

How well do you know the company you work for?
Chances are, you've never seen its articles of incorpora-
tion or charter, but should you examine them, you might
find a commitment from your company to society.

As citizens, legislators, and the media put pressure on corporations to take greater responsibility for the effects they have on
the community and environment around them, many companies are enshrining their commitment to social responsibility in
a charter. What's more, many companies agree to improve the
world around them in exchange for lucrative tax benefits (think
environmental regulation). And lots of companies these days
have established charity partners and bylaws that promote volunteerism. For example, some companies will match the funds
you raise for a charity, and some will make an annual contribution to any charity or nonprofit for which you volunteer.

The rise in corporate activism and nonprofit funding reflects the growing desire of corporate entities to be seen as positive contributors to the country. Social responsibility can shore up a company's brand image and even attract loyal workers. Still, corporations are merely a collection of people, often busy with their primary goal of maintaining profitability. It's up to you to help realize the promise of your company's charter and take the corporation up on its willingness to serve humanity. Call your company's human resources department or inquire at corporate headquarters about charity partnerships and funding deals to encourage volunteerism.

Finally, use your company as a platform to launch volunteer projects. Once an employee organizes an event for a charitable cause, most companies will hop on board with financial and organizational help. Corporations have the strategic and managerial skills to pull off events, fundraisers, and large projects that go well beyond the ability of a single individual. By getting your employer involved in a great cause, you'll be able to make an even bigger difference. Check out the Business for Social Responsibility Web site at BSR.org to find out great ways to get your company involved in your community.

TWENTY-NINE

Start a Book Club

The best way to keep your mind young is to constantly engage it. Reading can boost your vocabulary, expand your imagination, and activate your hunger to learn at any age. And, by starting a book club, you can reap all the benefits of reading while gaining a lot more.

These days, book clubs aren't just about the books; they're about community and getting neighbors together. Here's what a great book club can do for you.

• By participating in a book club, you become part of a scheduled event that provides the kick in the pants we all often need to finish a book in a timely manner. A book club is a great way to ensure that you read and to keep you reading regularly.

• A book club naturally broadens your reading horizons, because other people often select what the group reads. You may discover that nonfiction isn't so bad, fall in love with a new author, or learn about a fascinating part of the world you had never considered studying.

• By sharing your thoughts and feelings about a book with others and by listening to the epiphanies they had or their qualms about a book, you will deepen your appreciation of an author's skill with words. It's not uncommon to be ambivalent about a book, then leave a book club meeting loving it. Discovering the many layers of a novel can help you reach new levels of enjoyment.

• Attending book club meetings allows you to spend an intimate evening with adults in your community. What a wonderful way to enjoy time with people of similar interests! You may meet a new best friend or other parents whose children attend the same school as yours. You may meet your next accountant, the next mayor, or your next jogging buddy.

• Participating in a book club and reading books critically and seriously is a wonderful way to be a role model for your children. Being exposed to a commitment to learning and reading is a gift every child should receive.

What does any of this have to do with citizenship, you ask? Everything. The essence of democracy is citizens getting together and sharing ideas freely. Before the days of television and radio, it was how all public debate occurred. We didn't need "talking heads" and television pundits to help us form opinions. We did it ourselves by discussing ideas with the rest of the community. A return to discussion is good for us individually, and it's good for America. Inevitably, a discussion about a book will move on to a discussion about life today and the issues we face.

How to start? Choose people you already know to join your club, or ask your colleagues and your spouse's, or hand out a flyer to all of your neighbors. Then all you have to do is meet—and that's the fun part. Alternate houses for meetings, cook food related to the book, or try every restaurant in town.

Ultimately, book clubs are just plain fun. Intimidated by serious literature? Start a "beach book club." Have an affinity for Agatha Christie? Start a "mystery book club." A great book club can delve into biography or science fiction or any other topic. It's up to you!

Helping the
Environment

When did *environmentalist* become a dirty word? The truth is, we are all environmentalists. Whether we're outdoorsmen who enjoy fishing or hiking, suburban homeowners who find solace in a backyard garden, or urban dwellers who just want some quiet, we all want to preserve our country's most beautiful landscapes, combat pollution, and ensure that we have clean water to drink and fresh air to breathe. Americans may disagree on the policy issues that dictate how we protect our environment, but not many of us are actually *against* the environment. And why would we be? The Earth isn't just our planet; it's our home.

There's probably no other major American issue that individuals can address on their own as effectively as helping the environment. Yes, government and corporations need to act in ways that promote our long-term environmental health. But if we all used more clean energy, were more efficient with our cars, said no to excessive packaging and waste, and committed to small changes around our homes, we could stop worrying about where our oil comes from, whether it's safe to drink the water, or if our energy bills are going to crush us next winter. Each of us has the power to create a cleaner, safer America.

- THIRTY -

Become Garbage Obsessed

This is an easy one: The less garbage we produce,
the less garbage is amassed; the fewer landfills we have
to create; and the less we have to worry about rotting,
nasty garbage contaminating our planet.

The Earth belongs to all of us; keeping it free of as much garbage as possible just makes sense. The planet is our back-yard; it's where our kids play; it's the air we breathe and the water we drink. Contaminating our world with garbage and creating massive landfills is devastating for everyone, so treat the planet with the respect it deserves.

Each of us can drastically reduce the amount of garbage we produce. Here are just a few simple ways.

• Get rid of the paper in your life. These days, all of your financial accounts are accessible online, so why not sign up for e-statements instead of paper statements? Likewise, pay your bills online and reduce the amount of paper you toss. Done properly, electronic payments are highly secure. Also, cancel the nonessential catalogs you get by mail.

• Compost. If you have a backyard, use it. About 30 percent of all garbage is organic, so you can cut your output significantly just by composting. Create a compost pile with one of the many composting bins on the market. Then put two trash cans in your kitchen, one for food scraps and one for paper and plastic refuse. Every few days, dump the food scraps, along with yard trimmings, into the compost bin. In a few months, you'll have rich compost soil to use in your garden. Check out CompostGuide.com for more tips on getting the most out of your compost pile.

• Recycle. There's no excuse for not recycling at home anymore. It takes no time and very little thought: Just set up a bin and start throwing all your cans, glass, and plastic into it. Your local sanitation workers will do the rest. Also, make sure your workplace is recycling; after all, in most states, it's the law. Today, the question isn't what can be recycled, but what can't. Everything from used motor oil and electronics to batteries and paint can be recycled and reused. Visit Earth911.org for more information on how to recycle just about everything!

• Battle excess packaging. According to industry estimates, product packaging makes up about one-third of America's garbage and accounts for $1 in every $10 we spend at the store. There are lots of ways to fight back; buying in bulk, choosing reusable or recyclable packaging, and avoiding products that are overpackaged are just a few.

THIRTY-ONE

Sign Up for Clean Energy

When some people imagine clean energy, they think
of awkward solar panels on their roofs, or worse,
windmills in their backyards.

Such people think that solar energy can't be trusted on a
cloudy day or that wind power won't work when the air is
calm. But the reality is that clean energy doesn't involve rear-
ranging your home, installing a new energy system, or
worrying about the weather. Using it is as easy as turning on
the lights or plugging in your computer; in other words, it's no
harder to get or different to use than the energy that normally
courses through your home. All you need to do is sign up.

You see, power companies get their energy from a number of
different sources: oil, gas, nuclear energy, and, yes, solar and
wind power. Many communities in America allow you to
choose from which source you want to buy your energy, so by
signing up for clean energy, you're simply telling your power

company to purchase the electricity for your home from clean sources instead of from oil, gas, or nuclear power suppliers.

What's the effect? Simple: When you sign up for clean energy, your local power company will take a larger share of its total electricity from huge solar-panel fields or massive wind turbines far from your home. The price difference between standard and clean energy? Increasingly negligible. Of course, prices vary by region, so you need to do your homework. And don't fear: You'll never go off the power grid.

Subscribing to clean energy is about more than making the air a little cleaner. It can strengthen our national security. Oil, natural gas, and coal are in limited supply, particularly within our own borders, and as we all know, prices for fossil fuels are surging. Switching to clean technologies for electricity reduces our dependence on oil imports from the Middle East.

Not convinced? The facilities of the U.S. Army, as well as Whole Foods supermarkets and Staples Pharmacies, are all powered exclusively by clean energy, displacing millions of barrels of foreign oil and drastically reducing noxious emissions in the air. Your local power company may already have a clean energy option; make sure you check that option on your power bill. Or go to SmartPower.org, the definitive clean energy Web site, to find out about all of the clean energy options in your state and how to power your home with renewable energy.

- THIRTY-TWO -

Buy Regional Organic Food

They are two of the hottest trends in the food industry:
organic foods and local farmers' markets. In fact, the
two go hand in hand.

Thanks to rising consumer interest in naturally grown foods, more than a million new acres of organic cropland have come into use in the United States since 2000. And the results are easily found. Supermarkets today offer organic foods not only in the produce section but also at the meat counter, in the dairy section, and even in the bakery. And farmers' markets, featuring the just-harvested produce of local farmers, are popping up in cities large and small. So what's all the fuss about?

• Health. Pesticide residue is found in more than three-quarters of nonorganic produce. More than 90 percent of all beef produced in America contains growth hormones, which are banned in Europe. E. coli and salmonella bacteria are rampant in the nonorganic beef and poultry found in supermarkets. Statistics like these are leading many concerned consumers to make the switch to foods raised more naturally.

- The economy. When you buy regionally grown food, your money goes directly to local farmers and food outlets; when you buy mass-grown farm products, most of your dollars go to distant corporations to cover the costs of distribution, transportation, and marketing.
- The environment. Nonorganic farmers use 12 billion pounds of toxic artificial fertilizers and 1 billion pounds of pesticides each year. The effects of these chemicals on groundwater, lakes, and rivers—not to mention our drinking water—are significant. Plus, the average nonorganic fruit or vegetable travels more than 1,500 miles to reach your local store, necessitating the use of immense amounts of fuel for transportation.
- Taste. Heirloom tomatoes grown in small numbers by a local farmer using organic methods and sold to you a day after picking are generally going to taste a whole lot better than lab-developed hybrid tomatoes grown on a massive farm and shipped across the country, ripening during transport. Don't believe us? Try a taste test—with a tomato, apple, peach, zucchini, or any other fresh local item.

We can choose to ignore how our food is grown or raised, or we can select foods produced with the health of everyone in mind. Check out LocalHarvest.org to find out about community farming and organics in your area, where the foods are available, and how to make sustainable food a priority in your life.

THIRTY-THREE

Drive E85

The skyrocketing cost of oil not only cuts deeply
into each of our pocketbooks, it also helps fund
several of the nations that pose the greatest threats
to our economy, safety, and security. Global oil is a
finite resource, and the United States—the world's
largest oil buyer—is paying big bucks to the
world's most politically hostile countries for it.

There is something you can do: Using ethanol instead of pure
oil and gasoline can drastically reduce our dependence on foreign oil. Essentially, ethanol is grain alcohol. It's made from
crops like corn. Not only can it reduce U.S. dependence on
foreign oil, it can also be a great way to support American
farmers, since ethanol production is estimated to increase net
farm income by more than $4.5 billion. Automakers now
even have cars on the market that run on an 85 percent

ethanol, 15 percent gasoline mix: E85. And it's the same price as regular gas!

Financial considerations aside, you can still rest assured that eliminating oil-based emissions is perhaps the single greatest change we can make to benefit the environment right now. And ethanol is a renewable form of energy that is nontoxic and about 80 percent cleaner than the gasoline it replaces.

• A 10 percent ethanol, 90 percent regular gasoline combination known as E10 can be used in any vehicle on the road. In fact, roughly 1 of every 8 gallons of gasoline sold in America contains ethanol, and most of it is in an E10 mix. Find out if your local stations have an ethanol mix; if they don't, why not encourage them to get it?

• Automakers now have cars on the market, called flexible fuel vehicles (FFVs), that are designed to run on E85. Currently, Chrysler, Ford, GM, Isuzu, Mazda, Mercedes, Mercury, and Nissan all make E85-compatible cars at little or no additional cost. FFVs are an excellent option for drivers in the current market because they can run on regular gasoline when E85 isn't available. In fact, FFVs drive smoothly on any combination of gasoline and E85. To find an E85 station near you, or to see if your car is E85 compatible, check out E85Fuel.com.

THIRTY-FOUR

Use Energy Star Products

Did you know that your house can produce twice as many greenhouse gas emissions as your car? It's true. The items in our homes are often among the most inefficient users of energy in the country—from every lightbulb and coffeemaker to every washer and dryer.

That's why the U.S. government created the Energy Star program, an initiative to promote greater energy efficiency in America. The Environmental Protection Agency sets efficiency standards for all kinds of household products and appliances and then gives them the Energy Star seal if they meet those standards. You can even buy an Energy Star house; look for one if you're in the market.

Energy Star products not only help the environment by using fewer fossil fuels and emitting fewer greenhouse gases, they also help national security by reducing America's dependence on foreign oil. Plus, using Energy Star products can save you big money on your energy bill: Depending on how many of these products you use, you could cut your energy costs by up to 30 percent. And whether you're buying a lightbulb, an air-conditioning unit, or a whole house, you can receive various discounts and tax incentives from the government to do so. Check out EnergyStar.gov for a list of products and appliances that are Energy Star certified and to find out about special incentives for buyers.

Also, take the Energy Star Change a Light Pledge, a commitment to replace just one lightbulb in your home with an Energy Star bulb. Everyone can do at least that. If every U.S. household replaces just one incandescent bulb with one that's earned the Energy Star label, the country will save $600 million in energy costs, save enough energy to light 7 million homes, and prevent greenhouse gas emissions equivalent to those from 1 million cars. See what you can do around your house with Energy Star bulbs and other products. Once you've made the switch, all you have to do is sit back and enjoy the light—which will last longer and save you cash. Now that's an easy way to improve the environment!

THIRTY-FIVE

Go on a Bird Watch

Believe it or not, counting birds is not just a hobby; it arms scientists with valuable data that could affect your health and local environment.

Participating in National Audubon Society bird watches helps to monitor the status and distribution of bird populations across the Western Hemisphere; charting the presence (or absence) of certain species can be an important way to measure the environmental health of an area for humans—from the safety of groundwater to the air quality. Local trends can pinpoint environmental threats such as contaminants or a scarcity of habitat.

But keeping an eye on the birds can do more than home in on areas of possible contamination; it can also help protect at-risk bird species and be an early warning system for avian diseases like the West Nile virus. So whether you consider yourself an expert birder or just a fan of feathered friends, the National Audubon Society provides lots of ways to get involved.

- Establish a new winter tradition this year by participating in the annual Audubon Christmas Bird Count held nationwide; celebrate the season with a hike and a bird count.

- Participate in the Great Backyard Bird Count, a four-day event for birders of all levels. Watch the birds in your area, log your results online, and help the Audubon Society get a sense of the numbers and kinds of birds across North America.

- Join Project Feeder Watch and observe the birds that visit your home, then send that information to Cornell University scientists to help them determine where birds are thriving and where they're not.

- Check out the Audubon at Home guidelines to help create a healthy yard for birds and other wildlife and to learn about bird-feeding basics, plants that are good for birds, and the best ways to teach your kids about birds.

- Find out which bird species in your state are on the Audubon's WatchList and learn how to put together an Avian Inventory and Monitoring (AIM) team.

For more information about all of these fun programs, check out these Audubon Society Web sites: Audubon.org/bird and BirdSource.org. You can be a citizen scientist in your own backyard.

- THIRTY-SIX -

Plant a Tree in Your Community

Almost everyone loves trees, but did you know that
trees can help people heal faster?

It's true. According to the International Society of
Arboriculture, hospital patients have been shown to recover
faster when offered a view with trees. And while trees certainly
benefit any landscape—whether lining residential streets, dotting urban areas, or in full resplendence in the forest—they are
actually important to our daily well-being.

Trees improve the quality of the air around us by absorbing
dust and other particulates. Their leaves also absorb noxious
gaseous pollutants, such as carbon dioxide, ozone, carbon
monoxide, and sulfur dioxide, before we ever inhale them. Plus,
trees protect us from the effects of the sun and from rain, hail,
and snow—which can wreak havoc on unprotected homes—
and emit clean oxygen for us to breathe.

If the health of people and the environment isn't high on your
list of concerns, perhaps your wallet is: Trees make economic

sense. A home surrounded by trees costs less to cool and heat. Neighborhoods with trees are often several degrees cooler than those in similar climates that don't have trees. In winter, trees can keep your house warmer by blocking high winds. Also, less water is needed in tree-shaded areas where the sun isn't constantly beating down on the earth below.

Besides, trees can enhance privacy, block objectionable views, and boost the value of your home. Unfortunately, these days, mass construction projects tend to wipe out all the trees in an area before creating new neighborhoods and buildings. That's why it's more important than ever to plant a tree in your community.

Check out the National Arbor Day Foundation online at ArborDay.org to find out more about planting a tree in your area or how to volunteer in an urban center. You can even donate funds to help the foundation replant trees in New Orleans. Trees also make great gifts and wedding favors; the Arbor Day Foundation can tell you how to plant a tree in someone's name as a gift, donate a tree in someone's honor, or memorialize a loved one by planting a tree. Make Arbor Day a true holiday this year—plant a tree.

37

Grow a Chemical-Free Garden

A garden is a terrible thing to spray! While no one
wants bugs, other critters, or fungi to destroy a perfectly
beautiful garden, chemicals aren't the answer. Pesticides,
herbicides, and fungicides are designed to kill—and they
can be lethal to more than plant pests.

Harsh garden chemicals kill beneficial organisms as well,
including butterflies, ladybugs, and bees, all of which help our
gardens grow and stay healthy. More troubling is that garden
chemicals can leach into the groundwater, where they can leave
a toxic residue that poisons fish, small plants, and waterfowl—
not to mention the well water so many rural and suburban
homes rely on. According to the Environmental Protection
Agency, a number of lawn pesticides contain carcinogens that
in large quantities can cause birth defects, gene mutations,
nervous system damage, or liver and kidney damage. Why

introduce that kind of toxicity into your own backyard and expose your children and pets?

The next time weeds have you tearing out your hair, don't turn to harsh chemicals that will eventually contaminate the environment and poison your garden, groundwater, and family. Many books, Web sites, and magazines offer tons of tips on how to grow a beautiful garden without toxic chemicals. Get one! You'll find clever, effective solutions such as these.

• Tired of yard critters, squirrels, and bunnies munching the tasty plants and grasses in your yard or vegetable garden? Dose your delectables with a large shaker of cayenne pepper.

• Get rid of any and all standing water in your yard, including birdbaths. Standing water is a breeding ground for all manner of insects and a potential West Nile virus incubator.

• To get rid of root nematodes and other gnarly vegetable garden pests, plant marigolds in your garden to repel them.

• Buy lots of ladybugs and watch as aphids and other buggy pests disappear from your yard.

• Make your own insect repellent. Try adding a pureed garlic clove or a tablespoon of liquid dish detergent to a gallon of water. Then experiment with concentrations until you find one that does the trick.

The right mix of natural repellents will be more than sufficient to shoo garden pests away, and you won't turn your backyard into a toxic wasteland! For more tips, ideas, and homemade solutions that won't hurt the Earth or your health, check out BeyondPesticides.org.

THIRTY-EIGHT

Build a Garden in the Sky

Each time a city building is erected, the grass in that
spot and trees that once reached up to the sky are
replaced by a swath of asphalt or a tar roof.

Add to that the construction of roads, parking lots, and yet
more buildings, and the total lost green space can have a very
real effect on a city's air temperature, air quality, and energy
costs. On a summer day in most American cities, a tar roof
can feel like the inside of an oven. But what if we could
replace the hot roof of each skyscraper or building in a city
with grass or a garden?

Whether it holds vegetable gardens, wildflowers, or meadow
grasses, a green roof can lower the temperature above a building by 60 degrees, which can reduce the building's energy costs
and, if used more widely, could decrease a city's total energy
costs, reduce power-plant emissions, and improve air quality
and public health.

But that's not all—green roofs are a great way to handle water management in urban areas with overwhelmed sewerage systems (green roofs soak up excess precipitation), provide sanctuaries for urban wildlife, and actually extend the life span of the roof itself. And green roofs do something else: They beautify the city—whether you're on the 3rd floor or the 30th. Now that's a crowning achievement.

The environmental nonprofit group Earth Pledge is promoting a Green Roofs Initiative. To learn more about how to create a green roof—and the benefits it will provide—visit their Web site at EarthPledge.com.

THIRTY-NINE

Develop a Transportation Plan

In this country, driving a car is the single greatest contribution we each make to pollution, according to the Environmental Protection Agency. It's ironic, then, that there are more vehicles registered in the United States than there are licensed drivers.

We Americans are never going to stop driving. Not only is it essential to our way of life, but we truly do love our vehicles and being out on the open road. Without question, though, we can drastically reduce car emissions and foreign-oil dependency.

Think about your household. How many vehicles do you really need? Does each adult in the household need a car? More to the point, does each teenager? Do you own a car that you almost never drive? Creating a household transportation plan reduces emissions and your contribution to the country's dependence on Middle Eastern oil. Here are some ideas to keep you moving with less.

- Choose your cars based on your household's total driving needs rather than on each driver's personal preferences. For example, a family might share one or two small cars for going back and forth to work, school, or the store and have one larger vehicle for family trips or carrying large loads.
- Check out the car-sharing services in your town. These services give you access to a car when you need it, but when you don't, someone else can use that car. With a "lending library" of cars parked throughout the area, sharing a vehicle doesn't have to be any less convenient than owning one. Check out CarSharing.net to find out what's available in your area—whether rural or urban. Or try carpooling. You'll get home even faster when you're cruising in the HOV lane.
- Sell extra cars. If you've been hanging on to a second or third vehicle for those rare occasions when you truly "need" it as a spare or for carrying cargo, reconsider your position. Think of the money you'll save on insurance, registration, parking, and maintenance by renting a car a few times a year instead. Or get the neighbors together to buy a "community" pickup truck for heavy cargo needs, then stick with a fuel-efficient vehicle the rest of the time.
- Drive a hybrid. These amazing cars come with huge tax incentives from state and federal government bodies, save you tons on gas, and can cut emissions by half. Go to HybridCars.com to look up all the incentives available to you.
- Avoid buying an SUV. Sport utility vehicles are attractive and popular, but if you're interested in safety, they aren't good

choices. The sense of safety and security driving an SUV may give you is often deceptive. SUVs are prone to rollovers, in which the occupants are three times more likely to be killed than are occupants of cars, and collisions of SUVs and cars account for the majority of fatalities in vehicle-on-vehicle accidents. Plus, with far fewer miles to the gallon, SUVs guzzle gas and foreign oil, cost more at the pump, and emit far more toxic emissions into the air than traditional cars.

• Bike to work. Toxic vehicle emissions and human obesity rates are skyrocketing, but you can reduce air pollution—and your waistline—by bicycling to the office. Any cyclist will tell you biking is fun and healthy and makes parking a dream. National Bike to Work Week is May 15–19. Take advantage of the warmer weather and extra daylight and give cycling a shot next May—or sooner!

• Take public transportation. Hopping on the subway or bus is a great way to avoid the stress of traffic and the noxious carcinogens you breathe while sitting in gridlock. When you're on the train or bus, you can read the newspaper or catch up on paperwork on the way to work, saving you time. Besides, walking, even just to and from the station or bus stop, is a great way to start your morning.

Whether the goal is to reduce the number of weekly trips made by car, get a more efficient and safer car, or take the plunge and go car-free, each of us can make a big difference by streamlining our transportation choices.

Influencing
Leadership

It's no secret that the United States is a politically polarized country these days. With near-even splits down party lines in the last two presidential elections, Democrats and Republicans increasingly hostile to each other in Washington, and political scandals and corruption charges leaving everyone pointing a finger at someone else, it often seems that our differences are insurmountable.

The truth is, though, that political war in Washington doesn't necessarily represent the mindset or desires of America. Polls make it clear that the vast majority of Americans share the same goals and wishes: to live in peace; have good jobs; raise healthy, happy families; pay fair prices; receive good educations; and, well, pursue happiness. And they would much rather have a government at peace than one at war with itself.

So how do we end the never-ending political battles? Let it start with you. Reject the notion that every important issue must be debated through the framework of Democrat versus Republican. What's so often forgotten in the midst of 24-hour news coverage and endless campaigning is that politicians—the city councilmen, the mayors, the senators, the president—are *our* employees. They work for us, not for their political parties. The more we citizens vote, write letters, and hold our representatives accountable, the more responsible they will act. But if we don't vote with forethought, don't demand accuracy from the press, and don't expect honesty from our leaders, we may just find ourselves in a different kind of country. The greatest truth of democracy is that it only works when it is asked to.

- FORTY -

Just Pick Six

Select the six politicians or community leaders you
think are most important to your life and interests, then
tape their names, addresses, phone numbers, and e-mail
addresses to your refrigerator. Your picks can include
anyone from the president of the United States to your
state's agriculture secretary to the superintendent of
your local school district; it's up to you.

Why six? Simply because it brings government down to a
manageable size. Trying to track *every* politician and civic
leader clamoring for your attention is next to impossible. But
six is a large enough number to encompass local, state, and federal governments and include leaders important to your
personal interests.

Made your choices? Follow them. Read about them, visit
their Web sites, get their newsletters, attend their meetings or

speeches (or watch them on television), and track their voting records and success rates. What do they do well? What are they missing? Most important, are they doing a good job of representing you and your needs?

With your Big Six enshrined on the fridge, you'll be reminded of your role as the boss of some of these representatives. You'll find it easier to write letters or e-mails to let them know your opinions on the issues as well as your assessment of their performance. You may be surprised at how the conversation starts flowing in both directions. And when that happens, you may just find that your convictions are bolstered—or challenged—by learning more about the other side of the issues. This will make you a more thoughtful critic, or admirer, of their work.

Most of all, you may find a renewed appreciation of the way the system works and, even better, the impact you can have on our country's civil servants.

FORTY-ONE

Have an Opinion

A few days prior to every major election, TV news
stations gather up groups of "undecideds" and pepper
them with questions about what each candidate
could say to earn their votes.

It's outstanding that people in this country are open-minded
enough to consider candidates from either party and be receptive to ideas from across party lines. But being undecided just
before an election may be an indication that some people don't
know their own minds.

Election season shouldn't be the time to ponder what issues
are important to you; rather, it should be the time to ponder
which candidates best represent your views on the issues that
are meaningful. Having an opinion on the issues of the day is
something that should happen throughout the year. Knowing
whether you think tax cuts are wise, if farm subsidies make
sense, or if stem-cell research is important to you means

establishing your own platform, regardless of who's in office or who's running for office.

Why is having an opinion important? Because the opposite is so harmful. When citizens tune out, when they become apathetic, disillusioned, or disconnected, it gives politicians, corporations, and the media the freedom to do as they please. Suddenly, scandals start happening, bad laws start being passed, and the dating habits of today's hot starlet become the stuff of news.

Commit to becoming a bit of a newshound. Whether you prefer newspapers, television, the Internet, or radio, stay abreast of current issues. Read opinion magazines to see what other people are thinking about, and create your own list of priorities. Remember: The best way to judge your officials' on-the-job performance is to know how they have handled the matters of greatest concern to you over the years—not how well they did in a speech a few days before being up for reelection. Likewise, evaluate new candidates based on their command of the issues you're passionate about, not on how telegenic they are!

- FORTY-TWO -

Show Up

How engaged are you in the politics of your community?
Do you ever grumble about how the city is run or
complain about the lack of services in your town
but think there's nothing to be done about it? If so,
it's time to get active—to get on your feet, out of
the house, and into the community.

Start by attending a city council meeting; most are open to the
public, and your city's Web site should have all the details
about where meetings are held and what you need to know
before attending. City councils are made up of members of
your community, not distant fat-cat politicians. Chances are,
the council will be receptive to your complaint. It may be that
the members simply had no idea that your neighborhood has
so many potholes or that the city buses aren't arriving on
schedule. A problem that may have been a thorn in your side

for months could be resolved in one evening among reasonable people. And if you find that you aren't given a fair hearing, well, then you know whom to vote out come election time!

Try attending local leaders' speeches as well. There are many ways to learn about the issues that confront your area, but none are as intimate as speeches or town meetings. Is the speaker passionate or merely circumspect? Is he giving a stump speech, or is he really addressing concerns earnestly? Does he look people in the eye, or is he evasive or defensive? Watching officials in person is the best way to get to know them and their positions.

Finally, go to a political rally or two. Being around people who are galvanized by a cause is a fantastic way to gain more perspective about your community. Often, the people who champion a cause know more about the local leaders than the average citizen—and frequently, they are blinded by their own fervor. But you will find that attending events designed to call attention to an issue will give you the best education you can receive on that subject, whether or not you agree with the opinions expressed.

When civic events are open to the public, take it as an invitation to get involved. Show up and stand up—for yourself, your family, your neighborhood, and your rights.

FORTY-THREE

Write a Letter to the Editor

Did you know that the "Letters to the Editor" column is one of the most widely read sections of a newspaper? It's true. While some people may flip past the opinions of the community, many others are reading—carefully.

Not only does the public turn to this section of the paper to get a sense of what concerns their neighbors, but local politicians and community leaders read the letters to the editor with a keen eye toward gauging public opinion. All of this makes the letters column one of the most effective public forums for making your voice heard.

A letter to the editor may simply be a means of showing people in your community that you share their values and concerns, or it may spark a grassroots effort to take action on a topic you care about. Is the fare provided by the local school-lunch program no healthier than junk food? A letter to the editor could be a great way to educate others about the problem. Does the city council consistently ignore a growing pothole problem in your town? A letter to the editor may get more politicians to take notice. Does the local newspaper always exclude your neighborhood's special events? Raise awareness among the community and at the newspaper itself.

Your voice has power. Airing a grievance, bringing up a new issue, or addressing a point made in a newspaper article are all ways of engaging with your community and taking action about a cause you feel deserves more attention. Here's how.

• When writing a letter to the editor, pay careful attention to the guidelines established by the newspaper. Papers often have strict length limits and specific addresses to which you should send or e-mail your letter for consideration.

• If you are referencing an article published in the newspaper, be sure to include the date of publication and the author.

• Get your best points in right away. This way, your letter will have immediate impact and will stand a better chance of catching the editor's eye.

• Don't be mean or make personal attacks. A letter to the editor is an opportunity to be constructive about a problem, not to indulge in character assassination!

• Spell check, grammar check, and let someone else read your letter before you submit it.

• Include your name (your real one!), address, and telephone number. The editor will probably contact you before publishing your letter.

FORTY-FOUR

Volunteer on Election Day

It all started in 2000 with a hanging chad. Then there was a recount and talk of butterfly ballots, and the next thing we knew, we were watching as the Supreme Court stepped in to decide who would be the next president of the United States.

For the following four years, there were discussions about better, computerized systems and smarter ways to vote. But in 2004, there were long lines in Ohio—in some places, the wait was 8 hours—and as voters gave up or the polls closed before they could vote, people started to wonder: Just what needs to happen to ensure that the principle of one person, one vote is preserved and protected?

We may all hope for the big solution to emerge through legislation or a really superb new invention, such as a software program that lets people vote on the Internet with perfect accuracy. But until that happens, the answer to better voting lies with us. Individuals can still have a substantial positive effect on the voting system. Volunteers are needed every Election Day to do everything from giving rides to voters to monitoring polling stations. What better way to ensure the sanctity of the most basic right of every citizen than to take that day off from work and volunteer your time for this amazing American rite? Here's what you can do.

- After the 2000 election, the People for the American Way (PFAW) Foundation created an Election Protection Coalition to help guarantee voters' rights at the polls. Coalition volunteers man phones to help people find their polling stations, monitor polling places to ensure that no group faces disenfranchisement or intimidation, and distribute literature to engage Americans in citizenship. Check out People for the American Way at PFAW.org.

- Sign up to be a poll worker with the U.S. Election Assistance Commission (EAC). Established under the 2002 Help America Vote Act, the EAC will connect you with the voting administrators in your area. If you have foreign language skills, you may be especially helpful. Check out the opportunities at www.eac.gov/poll_worker.asp.

- Close to Election Day, the people at VolunteerMatch.org set up ElectionMatch.org and list all election-related volunteer opportunities in your area, including providing transportation to the polls.

- FORTY-FIVE -

Wear Purple on Election Day

Are you sick and tired of politicians hurling invective at the opposing party? Do you live in a Red state and vote Blue? Do you live in a Blue state and vote Red? Have you heard too often that the deficit is always the fault of the big-spending Democrats or the tax-cutting Republicans? Ever notice how the two political parties always blame each other for everything that's wrong with the country?

Sometimes political finger pointing can be exhausting. And the last time we looked, plenty of bad legislation and sly tricks were emerging from both sides of the aisle.

If you're like most Americans, you fall somewhere in the great center. The majority of people in this country are moderate, as evidenced by the fact that roughly 40 percent of us declare ourselves independent of any political party. Yet most

Americans feel herded into one camp or another. Somehow, politics in our country has become like professional sports, in which every action is measured in terms of which team won and which team lost.

Imagine, though, what it would be like if the best people from each party emerged via fair-minded elections to create a single team that worked together on the nation's behalf. It sounds simplistic, but America has experienced times in which the needs of the nation came before the rivalries of its political parties—and times like these can happen again.

So this Election Day, defy the conventional wisdom. Leave your Republican reds and Democratic blues at home and spend the day in your comfort zone: in the middle ... in purple. Wear regal purple this November to make a statement. Show your leaders—vividly—that no matter how much finger wagging they do or how many conciliatory promises they make, you stand for a united country. Show them that this us-versus-them stuff just isn't working. You belong to a wise America-loving majority that knows that no one party is responsible for every ill, and no one person is responsible for every success.

Make your representatives campaign to all of us, not just the party faithful. And let your representatives know, by wearing purple, that you won't be subject to convenient labels.

- FORTY-SIX -

Vote

It sounds so obvious, doesn't it? Yet many of us—*many of us*—are not voting at all. Well, maybe not at all: One in 10 adult Americans voted for the American Idol at least once during the 2006 television season, and a staggering 63 million participated in the final American Idol vote.

It's true that voting by phone or computer is much simpler than leaving home or work on a blustery Tuesday in November, but voting is a worthwhile effort because what's at stake is so much greater than who will be the winner of a TV talent competition. The process is necessarily stricter, more intentional, and more deliberate: Choosing the leaders of our country requires it.

One day, there may be a way to vote by phone or Internet at your leisure with complete accuracy. Until then, the process of voting outside the home will continue to ensure one vote per person and the highest degree of accuracy. Convenience—or lack of it—is not a reason not to vote. A democracy is only as vibrant as its citizenry, so think of voting as part of your job as an American.

Many people say that nothing ever changes, so why should they vote? But things *do* change: Supreme Court justices are selected; legislation on immigration, health care, taxes, and education are voted on; wars are waged; Social Security and Medicare are revised; and every day, new bills, propositions, and laws are discussed, proposed, and decided upon. The leaders and legislators chosen by the people are behind those changes, and it's up to you whether or not you are part of that. Are you electing the most responsible people? Are you using your vote to empower changes in your community? Here's how to learn how to be a great voter.

• Project Vote Smart is perhaps the single best Web resource for voters. At Vote-Smart.org, you can find biographies of the candidates running in your area and around the country along with concise summaries of their platforms, campaign finances, interest-group ratings, and voting records. Arm yourself with the basic knowledge you need to make a responsible decision at the polls. Spending a few minutes at Vote-Smart.org could mean the difference between a smart vote and a guess.

• Rock the Vote is still an amazing resource for young voters and first-time voters. Their Web site, RockTheVote.com, is chock-full of information about issues that affect young people, from student aid legislation to health care for twenty-some-things. Rock the Vote will also help young people maneuver the ins and outs of registering to vote, whether they live at home, are in college or grad school, are studying abroad, or are doing an internship in a new city.

• Voting may require you to make a stop at a local venue, but registering to vote is easier than ever. No matter your age, go to YourVoteMatters.org and make your voice heard.

Bettering
the Economy

Viewed through one set of glasses, our economy is extraordinary. Our country is wealthy, abundant with resources, and incredibly innovative. Seen through a different set of glasses, our economy is teetering on the edge of disaster. Massive budget deficits, trade imbalances, and huge personal debt levels threaten our future stability and well-being.

Which is the real U.S. economy? Easy: It's whichever one we choose. That choice, though, is one we must make not just in our minds but also through our actions. Whether we're talking about the federal government or a family in Idaho or a small business in Tennessee, the path to economic prosperity involves carefully tending to our cash, limiting waste, spending wisely, and investing for the future.

That's easy to say, but the truth is that too many of us let our hard-earned cash slip through our fingertips for everything from high-interest credit cards and indulgent evenings out to just poor planning. It's easy to think that the more you spend, the better off the U.S. economy will be, but that's just not so. It's far better for the country for each of us to be prudent, sensible money managers with an eye to the future. Our long-term prosperity is also America's future prosperity, so become an active and engaged participant in your household's economy. Remember, no one but you is looking out for your financial success. Take the job seriously.

- FORTY-SEVEN -

Limit Pleasure Shopping

In order to stay dynamic, a healthy economy depends
on people spending money. The problem is that we are
spending more than we can afford, and all that does
is create debt.

Now, debt isn't bad when it represents an investment in the
future, like a home mortgage, car loan, or student loan. But
when we go into debt for things we quickly use up and forget,
it's a danger sign—for both individuals and the economy as a
whole. And the signs are dangerous indeed.

Today, Americans have roughly $735 billion in credit card
debt—equal to $12,000 for every household that carries a cred-
it card balance. Credit has become so simple to get that people
think that they have somehow "earned" it or that if they are
"qualified" for credit, they are able to take it on.

That thinking is flawed. Credit should be used as tool to manage big expenses, such as a new refrigerator or a home

computer—important household items that you can afford to pay for in installments but not all at once. Credit should not be an easy way to drop $500 on new clothes, CDs, eating out, or groceries. Your paycheck should cover basic living costs.

Deep down, we all know this, yet a host of powerful influences, including advertising, the media, boredom, the Internet, and even peer pressure, have turned shopping into a favorite American pastime. Where once we might have gone to a movie or played a game for pleasure and relaxation, we now go shopping for its own sake and spend money we too often don't have. Meanwhile, we are maxing out our credit cards, facing escalating interest rates, and declaring bankruptcy in unprecedented numbers.

Make shopping something you do to fulfill your basic needs, not a reward or a remedy for boredom. Reining in frivolous spending may not seem significant compared to some other things in your life, but it may be one of the more important things you do for your family and your country.

Limiting pleasure spending can be very difficult, particularly if you've grown accustomed to it. Here are some guidelines for knowing when you can afford to pleasure shop.

- You have little or no credit card debt.
- After paying the mortgage or rent and making any loan payments (almost all of us have them, for car loans or student loans, for example), you have plenty of cash left over.
- You have plenty of money already set aside for your children's college educations and your retirement.

FORTY-EIGHT

Shop Mom-and-Pop

We live in a country of total convenience.

From bulk grocery stores to mega-bookstores and retail outlet shops, we can get everything we need faster and cheaper than can people in any other country on the planet. But as we spend more and more of our disposable income at huge chain stores and consumer products manufacturers, we do so at the expense of the great boutiques, shops, and specialty stores that have made American culture, food, and fashion so wonderful.

"Mom-and-pop shops" is a romantic but inaccurate term for all the entrepreneurial startups launched as a high-risk dream to provide consumers with better services or products. When we shop at them, we not only get unique products but also invest in our future economy. Each small business just may be the next big thing, whether it's the latest idea in food service or the hottest trend in sneakers. Supporting small businesses ensures that Americans will keep creating, innovating, and pursuing their own American dreams. Besides, mom-and-pop shops provide both unique characters and personal service; they'll tailor an order to your needs or tailor a suit to fit you perfectly. You can experience the fun of story hour at the mystery book shop, check out novelty shops for quirky gifts, listen to local musicians' latest releases, taste a truly fresh new flavor, or choose from a selection of thousands of hot sauces from all over the world. You can't do any of that at most malls!

By all means, purchase your everyday necessities in bulk, but the next time you need to buy a present, a loaf of bread, a book, or a shirt, head for a locally owned shop. Your purchase may cost an extra dollar or two, but you'll get a unique product and extra service, and you'll help a neighbor achieve a dream. Just as good, you'll help your community. Instead of shuttling so many of your dollars to companies and investors headquartered in other states—and frequently, other countries—you keep them in the community, which in time creates jobs, brings in new businesses, and helps your local retail economy thrive.

- FORTY-NINE -

Pursue Health

It may seem strange, but going on a diet, exercising a few times a week, and generally living a healthy lifestyle is one of the best things you can do to help the U.S. economy.

Imagine for a moment that the majority of American adults became fully committed to a healthy lifestyle. The number of diabetes cases would plummet. Heart disease would no longer be the leading cause of death. Think of all the heart bypass surgeries alone that could be avoided, and imagine the amount of prescription medicines we take dropping by half. Instances of cancer of all kinds would drop as eating foods rich in antioxidants, getting regular exercise, and using sunscreen all became part of our everyday routines. The lower incidence of cancer would mean fewer biopsies and less chemotherapy and radiation treatments for loved ones. Health care itself might become affordable, and doctors might be more available.

In a country full of healthy people, we might be more attentive to the elderly, more focused on finding a cure for countless diseases, and more effective in caring for those with legitimate medical needs. Health care costs might actually go down for employers if malpractice insurance and the escalating costs of tests and procedures became a thing of the past. And if those costs decreased for businesses, employers might hire more employees, better retain the ones they have, and generally grow the economy more through higher productivity.

All this, merely by living more healthfully. And the thing is, healthy living isn't just good for America; it's the best possible way of life for you and your family, too. When you feel great, and your loved ones are healthy, what's not to like?

Following a healthy lifestyle is easier than most people think. Relatively small changes quickly accumulate. To get you started, here's a list of the lifestyle tweaks that one panel of doctors says will have the most impact.

- Eat whole, natural foods rather than processed foods.
- Stop eating out of boredom, stress, or habit.
- Eat fish twice a week.
- Take a multivitamin with minerals every morning.
- Walk for 30 minutes a day.
- Quit smoking.
- Take 5 minutes a day to close your eyes and relax deeply.
- Talk to a friend every day—in person, on the phone, or via e-mail.
- Get a good night's sleep—every night.

- FIFTY -

Stay Out of Court

The United States is the most litigious nation in the history of the world. Instead of problem-solving or working out issues among ourselves, Americans are suing first and pondering the consequences later.

What no one is taking responsibility for is the economic effect of so many lawsuits, which is devastating. If you want to do something about government deficits, the economy, the cost of insurance, and even the cost of consumer products, just stay out of court.

Some people think the courtroom is the proper place to take any beef, no matter how petty, embarrassing, or absurd. According to the editors at Overlawyered.com, litigation too often acts as a weapon against the guilty and the innocent alike. It erodes individual responsibility and enriches its participants at the public's expense. The message in the country right now seems to be that if something bad happens to you, it must be someone else's fault, and you must be owed financial compensation.

This idea is not only ridiculous, it affects all of us. Our society has become so sue-happy that the average federal district judge fields 400 new cases a year. With dockets so clogged with junk, it can take years for legitimate cases to wend their way through the courts. Justice delayed is justice denied.

All of these lawsuits hit our wallets, too. Insurance premiums skyrocket as everyone scrambles to cover their behinds, court costs rise, and astronomical settlements depress corporate earnings and stock values. According to a White House Council of Economic Advisers estimate, the United States suffers an excessive "litigation tax" of $136 billion per year. Other experts put that figure even higher. Meanwhile, personal injury lawyers—whose smiling faces are visible everywhere on ads encouraging us to join the lawsuit parade—are laughing all the way to the bank.

So the next time your neighbor mows over your flowerbeds, you trip and fall at the supermarket, or you find yourself the victim of a practical joke gone wrong, remember that you are an adult. You don't need a judge to act as a parent and work out every dispute you encounter. Think about whether you've really been harmed or are just annoyed, and then try to work things out with the other party. Society shouldn't have to pay for silly accidents, petty grievances, and impetuous finger-pointing.

- FIFTY-ONE -

Watch Your Vices

Sometimes the greatest costs to our society come from
poor choices made by otherwise good people.

Unfortunately, our vices can quickly evolve into an overwhelming economic burden. Everyone loves having a good
time, but when occasional excesses become habitual, our nation
pays the price. Consider the impact of the usual assortment of
vices: drinking, gambling, and smoking.

• *Drinking.* In 2000, more than 2.1 million automobile crashes
in the United States involved alcohol, according to the
National Highway Traffic Safety Association. They killed nearly 17,000 people and injured more than half a million more.
What's more, the cost of alcohol-related crashes in the United
States that year was more than $114 billion—the lion's share
of which was paid by tax dollars. Plus, drunk-driving accidents
lead to many other indirect costs: higher insurance rates,
greater emergency health care needs, and the need for more
cops on the road. This is a monumental burden.

• *Gambling*. Much like a casino itself, gambling presents a slick façade: It seems to bring jobs to the community, generate revenue, and stimulate the local economy. Unfortunately, shrouded by these glittery promises is a darker reality. For many, gambling is addictive, and for those people, it's highly destructive. Gambling communities often experience higher rates of addiction, child abuse, domestic violence, suicide, crime, corruption, and bankruptcy. What may at first seem like a boon to the local economy can quickly become a losing proposition for taxpayers as higher law enforcement, social welfare, and regulatory costs become the norm. And now Internet gambling threatens to eat up the credit of the 8 million Americans who wager online each year. Add that to our already great credit woes, and it's a recipe for disaster.

• *Smoking*. Tobacco use remains the single leading cause of preventable deaths in the United States, killing 440,000 people each year. According to the Centers for Disease Control and Prevention, the total direct medical cost of smoking to our society is $75 billion yearly. Americans spent $82 billion on cigarettes in 2005; think of all the ways that money could have been better spent.

As we said, no one is against having a good time. But ask yourself this question the next time you partake of a vice: What would it mean for America if a million people did what you are about to do? If the answer scares you, that's a signal to rein things in—for you most of all, but also for your family, friends, and country.

- FIFTY-TWO -

Create a 401-Kid Plan

*In the past five years, youth spending has ballooned
to nearly $200 billion per year.*

Teens and even younger children carry cell phones. They eat
out with their friends at the mall and at fast-food places. They
buy the latest gadgets: iPods, digital cameras, and computers.
As a result, marketers have zeroed in on "tweens," kids roughly 8 through 12, who have graduated from buying just
bubblegum and Twinkies to purchasing music downloads, video
games, and even designer wardrobes.

We grownups usually pride ourselves on our sensible spending habits. By its very nature, though, much of youth spending
is frivolous. And to be blunt, excessive spending is first learned
at home. All hardworking parents just want to give their children the very best, but without the lessons of fiscal
responsibility, children learn how to spend, spend, spend. Start
teaching financial planning right from the start. Here's how
our 401-Kid Plan works.

1. Give your child an allowance. How much you choose to give is up to you as long as you can afford it, and it doesn't make your child feel like Paris Hilton! Many parents tie the amount of allowance to chores, which is a great way for children to get an understanding of work and the value of their time.

2. Tax the allowance. First, hand your child the allowance in its entirety so he can appreciate the full amount, then ask for 5 percent back. It won't make much of a dent in the sum, but it will teach your child about overhead. Instead of paying for education and sidewalks the way adults do, children can see their taxes go toward household expenses. Snacks, mortgages, and flute lessons aren't free!

3. Donate 5 percent of your child's allowance to a charity of her choice. Introduce your kid to great children's organizations such as UNICEF and St. Jude's Children's Research Hospital and mail off 5 percent of the allowance each month. Or visit a local shelter or nonprofit group and let your child donate in person. Teaching children the value their dollars have to others gives them a reward that will stay with them through life.

4. Finally, have your child put 10 percent of each allowance into a savings account—her own 401-Kid. Your child will learn about saving for the future and may decide on a goal to work toward. You may even be inspired to match the funds.

Before sending children off into the world, where offers for credit cards and quickie loans lurk around every corner, teach your children the value of a buck. They just might learn a little responsibility and smart decision making, too.

FIFTY-THREE

Be an Active Stockholder

Often, it seems a day doesn't go by without troublesome tidings about some major U.S. corporation.

At worst, it's news of major fraud being discovered or wending its way through the courts. Then there are the reports of lay-offs, of work being transferred overseas, of retirement benefits being slashed. Okay, you think, they're doing what they need to in order to stay healthy. But then you suddenly hear that salaries for top executives have jumped. It makes most Americans furious.

What we don't realize is that many of us need to take partial responsibility for how our corporations behave. That's right. When people purchase shares in a company, they have rights and duties not unlike the rights and duties we all have to our country. What a citizen is to a nation, a stockholder is to a company.

Once a year, for example, via an impartial election, you help to choose new corporate directors and make decisions about how the company is run. At annual shareholder meetings, you can ask questions about corporate strategy and challenge policies or executive pay. Plus, several times a year, shareholders receive official reports on all aspects of the company's business.

In other words, stockholders have the tools to change the leaders and operations of U.S. corporations. Just like being an active citizen of a country, being a shareholder of a company obliges you to be a participant. The price of passivity, after all, is too high: With out-of-control fraud, waste, and ineffective management, unethical corporations can put thousands of people into financial turmoil.

So vote each year when you get your proxy. E-mail questions that you'd like answered at the annual shareholder meeting as well as any questions or concerns you have as news emerges in the business world. Read all of the materials you are sent, such as the annual report and proxy, and share your responses with the company—and if you wish, with other large shareholders. Let the corporate world know that you own a piece of the pie and that you are watching, that you expect integrity and openness, and that in return, you will give your loyalty and support—and continued investment dollars. Check out CorpWatch.org to find out more about keeping corporations honest and accountable.

FIFTY-FOUR

Save for the Future

*Don't wait to start putting aside money for your
child's college education, and don't start in your fifties
to save for your retirement. Saving money and
keeping debt levels low are your very best insurance
for a happy and stress-free future for you and your
loved ones. Prudent saving—not unchecked spending—
is better for our country as well.*

We all know this deep down—and yet Americans have made
accumulating debt a national pastime. We consumers owe
retailers and lenders more than $2 trillion, and the amount is
growing fast. Too many of us are putting ourselves at risk of
becoming wards of the federal government in our senior
years. With the future of the Social Security system in question, and health care programs like Medicare uncertain, how
sensible is that? Eliminating debt and creating a smart fiscal

plan is the best way to protect yourself and your loved ones in the future.

Saving should become a natural monthly habit—like paying rent or making your car payments. Here are some easy tips to make the most of your savings and help eliminate debt.

• Put 10 percent of every paycheck into savings. You can set up a college savings account, a money market account, or a Roth IRA, but however you choose to store your money, make sure that you do not touch it. Grow your money through interest; make your savings accounts untouchable!

• If your employer offers a 401(k) program, sign up for it now. 401(k)s are excellent ways to maximize your salary tax-free and to create a shelter for your retirement funds. Try to put the maximum allowable amount into your 401(k).

• "Tax" yourself on luxury goods: Every time you make a luxury purchase, put 10 percent of the price into savings. Thus, those $400 high-fashion Jimmy Choo shoes will mean tucking away $40 for the long term; that new $300 golf club will net you $30 in savings. It may not seem like much, but by the end of the year, you may find that you've saved hundreds or even thousands of dollars. Over time, that will accrue and may mean you'll be able to retire a year early or at least be able to buy your son's college textbooks!

• Formal savings programs are essential, but don't pass up sensible everyday savings opportunities. For example, every night, put a dollar in a jar along with all the loose change in your pockets, wallet, or purse. You may not notice a dollar and change missing at the end of every day, but at the end of the month, you'll see impressive savings. At the end of the year, you could have an extra $500. Just make sure you deposit the money in the bank—otherwise, dipping into the jar may be too tempting! Use the cash to pay down credit card debt or bulk up your savings.

The bottom line: Protect yourself from debt, and keep an eye on your financial future. You may find that a little frugality today can go along way toward ensuring the sanctity of your life tomorrow.

Ending
Hatred

After the attacks on the World Trade Center and the Pentagon on September 11, 2001, we Americans made some promises. We were going to read up more on international affairs, we were going to try to better understand foreign policy, and we were going to seriously consider our role on the larger world stage. Post-9/11, we understood that something needed to change, that we had not been acknowledging a serious and existential threat. Yes, we committed ourselves wholeheartedly to battling terrorism, but we were also resolutely inspired to end hatred at home and abroad.

America remains fully engaged in the battle against terrorism and will for as long as it takes to win. But how many of us have fulfilled that other promise, to do battle

against bias and hatred? How much do we as a country follow international politics or reach out to other cultures? Maybe we just weren't given enough of an idea of what each of us could do in our own lives to create a country that teems with tolerance and is recognized the world over for its compassion, charity, and warmth—for it's certain that America is all of these things.

Luckily, there are many ways each of us can engage the nations of the globe and enrich our own lives. And by taking the steps to end hatred, we will also take the steps to quell the fervor of our foes. Ultimately, in the act of reaching out, we may discover a greater truth: To be an American is also to be a citizen of the world.

Reconnect With Your Roots Overseas

Almost every one of us can trace our background
to another country.

Sometimes we forget this. For some of us, our family migrations occurred several generations back. For others, mixed-culture marriages by parents and grandparents have diluted connections to any single heritage. Sometimes, painful memories encourage us to disconnect from our personal histories, and sometimes, we just get caught up in the present.

We can choose to ignore or forget our family heritage, but at what price? Our cultural origins are as real as our American childhoods. Celebrating our connectedness to the larger world is a perfectly American thing to do. Not only does it provide each of us with pride and history, but as residents of the most diverse nation on Earth, we can best show the world what harmony among cultures can look like. So take pride in your country and take the time to reconnect to your roots overseas.

How to start? Ask your parents, uncles, aunts, and cousins for leads that will allow you to locate distant family members. Then make an introductory contact, probably with a letter. Find out if they have e-mail. Exchange photos. Let it progress naturally. Will a phone call be next? A visit?

You needn't limit this to family. If you are a veteran, are there people you encountered during your tours of duty that you still think of? Are there exchange students with whom you were once friends? Coworkers from overseas who have moved back home? It is an amazing blessing to have an extended circle of family or friends living in other parts of the world, in another culture. Through them, you can learn much about life elsewhere—and they can see and learn more about American life in return.

Even if you don't have any overseas connections, think about the nations and continents that are part of your being. How different is life in Africa from that in your suburban neighborhood in Dallas? How would your life be different if you had been raised in China? What if your family had remained in El Salvador? What are the daily priorities of your Scottish cousins? If you can, take a trip to a region of origin for you and discover what traditions may have been huge parts of your relatives' and ancestors' lives. You may find that reconnecting to your roots will influence your life in America in meaningful ways.

FIFTY-SIX

Eat at an Ethnic Restaurant

Nothing introduces you to a culture better than visiting
one of its restaurants and experiencing its food.
Whenever the opportunity arises, dine with your family
at an ethnic restaurant.

It's not that hard to do. How many times each month do you
find yourself mindlessly veering toward the same ol' restaurants for the same ol' hamburgers or pizza or fried chicken?
Don't get us wrong: There's nothing wrong with a plate of
your favorite comfort food every now and then. Once in a
while, though, try avoiding the usual suspects and take your
family out to a Thai, Mexican, Indian, Japanese, Brazilian, or
any restaurant at all that's different from your normal haunts.

You may find, for example, that a falafel platter with all the
trimmings and a side of hummus is not only delicious but
also offers you the opportunity for a more honest view of
the Middle East than you'll get from a newspaper. Ethnic

restaurants in America are often run by the hardworking immigrants who have always made this nation great. Introduce yourself to the owner and find out how his American dream came to life in your town. You may learn that the curry paste on your lamb is his grandmother's recipe, that the pictures on the wall are of his hometown, that the music playing in the background is a huge hit in his country, that his daughter attends the same local high school as yours, and that imported beer tastes best when shared with a native connoisseur.

Ethnic restaurants are tucked into most corners of our suburban and urban landscapes nowadays. Take advantage of them. Each one offers us the opportunity to discover not only new and wonderful food but also good people representing the full spectrum of cultures in our country—and the world. It is an easy, positive first step toward more understanding and tolerance. Besides, you'll get to eat some fantastic dishes—like pad Thai, pulled-pork tacos, vegetable tempura, chicken tikka masala, corn-husk tamales, Ethiopian lamb stew, shish kebabs and couscous, seafood frittatas, tabbouleh....

57

- FIFTY-SEVEN -

Look at a Map

A 2006 National Geographic survey found that despite
two wars in those countries, most young adults could
not find Iraq or Afghanistan on a map.

Not good, but perhaps not so surprising. But what about the fact
that despite the onslaught of Hurricane Katrina and months of
media coverage, only one-third of those surveyed could find
Louisiana on a map? It seems that America is failing geography.

A lack of understanding about our physical place in the
world and about where our interests, our troops, or our allies
are located keeps us isolated mentally, adrift in our American
paradise with no sense of where anyone else is. It's a detri-
ment to America not only with regard to our educational level
but also because we are a world leader, depending on our relationships with other countries to create peace and enforce it
wherever possible around the world. Our economic ties to and
environmental concerns for the rest of the world also bespeak

the importance of having an understanding of our globe that goes beyond our own state or county.

Learning about geography entails not just learning where places are but also why they are there, how they came to be, and what characterizes them. Geography is about understanding the world, not just naming its parts.

It's not that important, you say. We beg to differ. In the increasingly competitive world marketplace, prosperity will come to those who reach out successfully to new markets. Our competitors in Asia and Europe are more than happy when U.S. businesses don't bother to learn about the emerging markets of the world. True, you alone can't change this, but when we collectively expand our vision, anything can happen.

Having maps or a globe in the house is the first and best way to start examining the layout of our Earth. Look up countries you hear about on the news and take a look at nearby countries and landscape. Let a map be your guide to opening your eyes to the world.

Talk to your children about the world. Have them spend time looking on a globe for countries important to the United States or to your heritage and culture. Find the countries your child's classmates come from and look at the distances between them. Look at how far it is from Alaska to Florida and then consider the distance between your house and the Mexican border or between Europe and the Sahara. Make understanding the neighborhoods of the world a regular activity in your home.

FIFTY-EIGHT

Sample Other Nations' News

The world has become a much smaller place than it used to be. Media has created a channel through which we can discover other cultures from the comfort of our own homes. Take advantage of this unprecedented stream of information and discover the news according to a foreign country.

Not only will you learn about the big topics in other countries, you'll also see how the world interprets the news happening here in the United States. It's a perspective that is often surprising, occasionally depressing, and frequently revealing. In particular, you may find yourself becoming a lot more critical of the job the U.S. media is doing!

Many Americans don't realize that most countries in the world offer English-language editions of their publications. Often, these newspapers or magazines are aimed at Americans and other English speakers living abroad, some are directed at expatriates, and still others are published specifically for an American audience to encourage us to take an interest in other cultures. It's an opportunity that's available every time you log on to the Internet. Check out World-Newspapers.com to find English-language press from around the globe. Find a country you are interested in and start reading.

Also, many cable television packages now include access to international stations. Watching any of the British Broadcasting Corporation productions—BBC News, BBC World, or BBC America—is sure to give you a taste of how Europeans see the news of the day and just what that news is for them. The BBC's focus is different from that of news stations and other programming in the United States, making BBC broadcasts excellent complements to your usual news routine.

Finally, to glean a truly unfiltered sense of what the rest of the world thinks of us, check out the amazing WatchingAmerica.com, a Web site devoted to translating foreign press from every corner of the globe without comment or distillation. Check out Iraqi newspaper articles, Venezuelan columnists, Chinese headlines, and Al Jazeera broadcasts—all translated into English. They are eye opening and profound. Learning about the world takes exposure to more than one country's media, so open yourself to the news of the planet— as well as news of America as seen through others' eyes.

FIFTY-NINE

Sign Up for a Sister City

In 1956, President Dwight D. Eisenhower initiated a program designed to create person-to-person contact between Americans and people from all over the world. That program is now known as Sister Cities International and this year is celebrating its 50th anniversary.

Sister Cities International helps to forge bonds between American communities and similar-size locales in other countries. Through these connections, Sister Cities has become a leader in increasing global cooperation, promoting cultural understanding, stimulating economic development, and sparking volunteerism abroad.

At Sister-Cities.org, you can find out if your area already has a sister city and if so, how to get involved. You can also learn how to sign up for an additional one; Sister Cities encourages multiple exchanges. Or you can request a first-time sister city, even if it's for just your neighborhood or enclave. You don't have to be the mayor to sign up for a sister city, although taking the idea to your city council or town meeting is a great way to get the entire community involved.

Having an international sister city is a wonderful way for a community to establish foreign business connections and unique educational opportunities. Once the match is made, a number of initiatives can begin.

• Teachers in your community can pair up with a sister school or classroom in the foreign community for special projects, and students can participate in programs such as attending the International Youth Summit on Global Citizenship or doing an exchange study program.

• Joint arts programs in music, dance, and crafts can begin. Your community can also participate in the Sister Cities International Young Artists Competition, in which young people from around the world share their talents.

• Direct participation in humanitarian assistance abroad can be a hallmark of your community with amazing Sister Cities partnerships with groups such as Wheelchairs for Peace, the Islamic Peace and Friendship Initiative, emergency response and preparedness programs for natural disasters, and Operation Iraqi Children.

Check out Sister-Cities.org to find out more, and get a toolkit and guide to help you and your community become global partners.

- SIXTY -

Get a Passport

Only 1 in every 4 Americans
currently holds a passport.

If you are one of those 70 million, we applaud you. If, on the other hand, you are one of the more than 200 million Americans who don't yet have passports, consider finally obtaining one and assuring yourself entry to the rest of the world.

Even if you have no plans to travel abroad right now, why preclude the possibility? Just having a passport is a way of making a statement: If a driver's license is your state I.D., then a passport is like an American I.D. Holding a valid U.S. passport is proof of nationhood as well as an implicit recognition of a larger world.

Besides, a passport comes with distinct advantages in the global economy. If you are in the business world, having a passport means you will never fear that last-minute trip to Asia. If you are just starting your career, having a passport is like injecting your résumé with a shot of skills and know-how;

employers love international experience, even if it's just travel. Even more important, holding a passport demonstrates an understanding that the United States does not exist in isolation, that you appreciate the intricacies and vastness of a bigger world. A passport is an indication of a willingness to learn, an intent to travel, and an eagerness to experience life beyond the familiar, to explore, and to be adventurous.

A person with no passport, on the other hand, conveys an image of isolation and a limited worldview. There is a lot of life outside our borders; chances are, you will love America even more after having a glimpse of the rest of the world. You will also have greater compassion and tolerance for others once you've seen a bit of life around the globe. As the great American writer and thinker Mark Twain observed, "Nothing so liberalizes a man and expands the kindly instincts that nature put in him as travel and contact with many kinds of people."

For information on how to obtain a passport—or renew your old one—check out the State Department's Web site, Travel.State.gov/passport. And if you need more reasons to think about a passport—or just crave some inspirational stories of people who ventured out of their comfort zones for the first time—consider buying the Lonely Planet book *Don't Let the World Pass You By! 52 Reasons to Have a Passport.*

SIXTY-ONE

Go to a Pro Soccer Game

If you're already on soccer patrol every weekend
with the kids, give them a treat and take the family to a
soccer game played by the pros. And if soccer isn't on
your radar at all, make a point of checking it out.
Although most Americans don't realize it, soccer is far
and away the most popular sport in the world.

Whether you're in South America, Europe, Africa, or Asia, soccer is the sport you'll see children playing at recess, after school, and in the backyard. And the game inspires a kind of unbridled fanaticism rarely seen in U.S. sports. Imagine the fervor of the Yankees versus the Red Sox in the American League Championship, then imagine that kind of spirit for every game of the baseball season. That's the intensity of the appeal that soccer has for most of the world, and the sport is quickly gaining in popularity here in the United States, with stars like Mia Hamm and phenoms like Freddy Adu capturing the public's imagination.

Most major cities in the United States now have professional soccer leagues, and making the effort to attend a match is well worth it. Soccer games attract many of the newest American citizens and people from all over the world. It's a truly fun way to learn about other cultures, the diversity here in America, and the thrill of being part of a throng of soccer fans. And don't be surprised if the crowd isn't rooting for the home team; in soccer, an individual player's nationality can trump the crowd's allegiance to a local team!

Soccer games are loud, raucous, fun, and incredibly athletic. Watching star players maneuver down the field with dazzling alacrity and dexterity just may give you a renewed commitment to that Saturday soccer league your child is so fond of. And you may also learn a thing or two about how the rest of the world likes its sports—served with theatrics, endurance, and patriotism. Go to a game and make friends with the diverse mix of people who happen to be there, then yell and cheer until your throat hurts!

SIXTY-TWO

Learn a Foreign Language

In most countries in the world, speaking more than
one language is common and even expected. Fluency
in another language is a sign of education, status,
and even business savvy.

In a world where mass transportation has made worldwide
travel routine, familiarity with other cultures and languages
is a surefire way to be seen as a good global citizen—and that
is indeed good for America.

Yet despite the fact that ours is one of the most educated
countries in the world, foreigners are routinely mystified by
Americans' lack of language skills. The idea that we don't have
to learn foreign languages because so many people abroad
speak English is not only inaccurate, it also isn't representative
of America. We Americans don't take the easy way out; we
strive to be better, smarter, and more knowledgeable.

Besides, learning a foreign language opens you to another culture in more significant ways than just communicating through words. Eating the food of that country, listening to its music, and even planning a trip abroad become natural consequences of your language studies. Plus, you may find that studying Chinese helps you in business, that learning Spanish gives you a new perspective on your neighbors, that speaking Arabic may mean being able to contribute to national security, that conversing in French leads to new friendships, and that having a basic knowledge of any language opens up a host of new career opportunities. And for young people, knowledge of a foreign language is shown to result in higher standardized test scores.

There are lots of great ways to learn a language. Check out a local college for adult education classes, start a foreign-language coffee group, or buy a series of the Rosetta Stone language tapes and make your commute to work an opportunity to take in a new dialect.

- SIXTY-THREE -

Go to Other Places of Worship

When growing up, children are often taught that theirs is the one true religion. We certainly wouldn't argue with such personal conviction, but believing wholeheartedly in your religion doesn't mean that other religions are not to be respected or learned from.

Our world today is ablaze with radical fundamentalism and misunderstanding. Ordinary Muslims are treated as harbingers of terror or sexism instead of as peace-loving souls devoted to family; everyday Jews are known more by mean-spirited stereotypes of greed and control than for the beauty of their ancient traditions and beliefs; and dedicated Christians are perceived as missionaries and social conservatives before they are even heard. And that's not to mention the general lack of awareness in this country about, say, Shinto beliefs, Hinduism, Zulu tradition, Mormonism, Sufism, Kwanzaa (not a religious holiday!), Buddhism, or any of the hundreds of other religions that are practiced in our country every day.

Why is this so? One big reason is that, when it comes to religion, the news media focus mostly on the shrill voices and destructive actions of religious extremists. Absent any other information, it's easy to develop unfair and inaccurate views of the true nature of other religions. And this hurts us all.

So try this bold but worthwhile task: Visit a local mosque, church, synagogue, or any other house of worship that you don't know much about. Many religious establishments are happy to answer questions, let you watch a ceremony or weekly rite, or even invite you to partake in a holy meal.

Call first, though, particularly if a large group wants to make a visit. Nowadays, many religious organizations have outreach coordinators who can arrange for you and your group to meet with their leaders. They'll also advise you on how to act when visiting—what to wear, for example, or when to be silent.

Perhaps the best first stop for anyone interested in discovering other religions is BeliefNet.com. This comprehensive Internet site is devoted to exploring the traditions and spiritual meanings of all religions, with advisers from every faith. Ask about parenting as a Jew or healing as a Muslim, or just read the thought-provoking columns and articles written by bright, articulate religious thinkers. You're likely to find that your open-mindedness not only helps your faith but also makes you a wiser, fairer person. And what religion—or country—doesn't want that of its people?

- SIXTY-FOUR -

Host an Exchange Student

We hear so much these days about anti-American
sentiment abroad. Every night, it seems the evening
news reminds us of ongoing anti-American or
anti-Western protests or even just the condescending
comments of a foreign ally. Do you ever feel that if only
these other citizens of the world could get to know us
as people, they might just see that Americans have
powerful spirits, strong values, and big hearts?

You can show the world just how warm and fun-loving
Americans really are by hosting an exchange student from
abroad. Giving a foreign student the opportunity to get to
know the real America and not the Hollywood version is one
of the best gifts you could give to our country. Promoting cultural and religious understanding by inviting a young person

into your home just may make the United States a little safer and more secure in the future, too.

Imagine sharing Halloween with a Russian teenager, watching Fourth of July fireworks with a boy from Pakistan, taking a Chinese youth to his first basketball game, or introducing a Kenyan girl to your favorite pizza joint. Our everyday lives are filled with awe-inspiring first-time experiences for students from around the world, who will go back home with stories of a wonderful American trip. What's more, seeing your own life through the eyes of someone new may just make you realize what a great country you live in.

The effects work the other way, too! You might make fried plantains with a Mexican student, have a tea ceremony with a Japanese teen, or learn how to write the letters of the Arabic alphabet. Whether you have young children or are retired with an empty nest, hosting an exchange student creates a lasting bond. You may find that people of different nations aren't so different after all. And who knows, one day you may receive an invitation to a wedding in a strange land or find that you always have a place to stay in South Africa or Ireland or India or Brazil.

If you have children, your kids will develop an amazing bond with an exchange student. Often, they quickly become like siblings or best pals, eager to play in the yard together, go to the mall, or just have silly conversations. With an exchange student in the house, your kids could even begin to pick up a foreign language or use their understanding of a new culture in classroom reports—and colleges love it when their prospective students have had this type of experience!

Most exchange programs place foreign students with excellent grades in U.S. homes. The organization sets the students up in school and provides medical coverage. Students have their own spending money, and host families can even receive tax deductions. For more information, check out these amazing programs.

- AFS (formerly known as the American Field Service) at USA.AFS.org
- Academic Year in America (AYA) at 1-800-322-HOST or online at AIFS.com/AYA

Believing in
America

Emotions are infectious. If one person is openly happy, the people around that person will soon become happier. If one person in a group is hostile, it doesn't take long for the atmosphere in the room to grow hostile. It's a fascinating part of human nature.

Opinions are the same way. All it takes is one person to stand behind a passionate, strong opinion, and others will gravitate to it as well.

Today in America, emotions and opinions about our country too often fall on the side of negativity. Yes, debate and skepticism are vital parts of our nation's personality, but glumness, hostility, and pessimism are not. It's time for a change—for *all* Americans to become excited about our nation again.

The greatest assurance of a thriving democracy is a passionate population. Don't love your country because you

happen to have been born here; love your country for its history, its tenets, its freedoms, and yes, its potential. Love your country enough to demand change, to speak out against bad legislation, and to argue or protest. Don't find yourself ambivalently muttering about a better past or romanticizing life in countries to which you have never been. Reclaim your zeal: Get excited about the potential of America—even if you think that means big changes have to be made.

After all, change is inevitable in the United States. For that reason alone, we all should be optimistic about our country's future. We live in a nation with a young, rich history and an indomitable and audacious spirit. Take part in this national adventure called America—and imagine the possibilities for tomorrow!

- SIXTY-FIVE -

Combat a Culture of Cheating

Pro athletes cheating by using steroids. Businessmen cheating by lying about the health of their companies. Reporters and authors cheating by plagiarizing or making up "facts." Politicians cheating by taking bribes and using donations improperly. Religious leaders cheating by betraying the trust of their congregations. Some days, it seems that the top category of news headlines is once-revered people who get caught cheating.

And it's hardly just the rich and famous. Students across the country have become experts at cheating by buying term papers, plagiarizing, and instant-messaging exam answers. There's a myriad of Web sites offering opportunities to cheat on your spouse. Forty-four percent of job applicants lie about their work histories, according to one large-scale analysis. And few people can seem to refrain from cheating on their taxes.

Cheating seems to stain almost every aspect of daily life today. It is to the point where many people even feel *entitled* to cheat. At what point did so many Americans decide that living in one of the most peaceful and freedom-loving countries on Earth meant that we deserve to take more than we are due?

Is this the America we want to live in? It's time to stop the culture of cheating that has pervaded our country, and the change starts with each of us. While integrity from the top down will make an enormous difference in every area of society, we are all ultimately responsible for ourselves. It's time to usher in a new age of honesty. Here's what you can do.

• Support legislation that combats cheating. Look at bills aimed at everything from steroid abuse to the discretionary power of the Securities and Exchange Commission, then sign petitions, write letters to congressmen, and throw your full support behind laws designed to curb cheating and promote fairness.

• Expect more from your leaders. Don't overlook allegations of corruption just because they come from the "other" party. Ask the tough questions of local and national politicians regardless of political affiliation. Make honesty and integrity crucial components of your voting thought process.

• Honor whistleblowers. No one should fear losing a job or facing ridicule for exposing cheating in the workplace. In your home and at your office, make speaking up for honesty a value that is championed.

• Support watchdog groups. Depending on the cause that's important to you—from veracity on product labels to health care fraud—there are tons of nonprofit watchdog groups and think tanks ready to inform you about the latest abuses in their field. Subscribe to a newsletter or donate to an organization.

• Get savvy about your kids' homework. Check their assignments and look out for suspicious phrasing or troubling facts. These days, cribbing material from the Internet is just a quick cut-and-paste away. Being a homework watchdog is the best way to ensure that your child learns instead of copies.

• Be an integrity hero. It's often up to you to make the small choices that contribute to an honest and fair society for all of us. Don't illegally download a movie or song, be quick to speak up when the cashier forgets to charge you for something, and behave with the kind of character you expect from others.

SIXTY-SIX

Memorize the Preamble to the Constitution

As mission statements go, the preamble to the Constitution of the United States is perhaps the most important and recognizable paragraph in the history of the nation—maybe even the world.

At a time when our nascent country comprised a collection of state governments, each with its own currency and tariffs, the Founding Fathers sought to unite our nation under a strong federal government that could ensure the well-being of its people; they sought a "more perfect union."

On September 10, 1787, Alexander Hamilton, William Johnson, Rufus King, James Madison, and Gouverneur Morris presented the final draft of the preamble to the Constitutional Convention. This sentence would become the beacon of liberty in a unified nation:

*We the people of the United States, in order to form a
more perfect Union, establish justice, insure domestic
tranquility, provide for the common defense, promote the
general welfare, and secure the blessings of liberty to ourselves and our posterity, do ordain and establish this
Constitution for the United States of America.*

We the people ... One of the greatest phrases our country
has ever known, "we the people" became an expression of
respect for the common man and a triumphant announcement
that the Constitution was not divinely inspired but created by
the people of this land.

To form a more perfect Union ... Without a strong central
government, the pre-Constitution states were beginning to
seem like distinct countries of their own, with no overarching
set of laws with which to govern. Our success in creating "a
more perfect union" is what separates us from other regions of
the world in which independent nations try but fail to cooper-
ate with each other.

Establish justice ... Creating a fair court system that would
act with uniformity throughout the states was of paramount
concern to the framers, who saw imbalances in trade and tariffs
from state to state.

Insure domestic tranquility ... The framers sought to ensure
that the federal government had the power to stymie infight-
ing and territorial disputes between the states in order to
preserve the cohesiveness of the country.

Provide for the common defense ... Where no one state was prepared to fend off an attack from outside the confederacy, a common army would be a potent force for the union.

Promote the general welfare and secure the blessings of liberty to ourselves and our posterity ... Through justice, domestic tranquility, and a common defense, the United States would be a place where the common man could pursue the benefits of stability and peace with unprecedented freedom—away from tyranny or monarchy.

In other words, the preamble to the Constitution laid out the magnificent promise of our country in just a sentence. So memorize these words and connect to the spirit of those who enshrined the freedoms we all share; tap in to the great adventure of your own history.

Need help learning it? Check out ConstitutionCenter.org for an explanation of the preamble and the Constitutional Convention as well as for games, exercises, and more facts about the Constitution and the men who wrote it. And if memorizing text is really difficult for you, go to SchoolhouseRock.tv and learn to sing the words of the preamble!

SIXTY-SEVEN

Reconnect With U.S. History

If you know American history well enough, it's almost impossible not to respect and cherish this country.

Yes, we should judge ourselves most by the realities of the present. By understanding how we got here, however, and knowing that many times in our past, we overcame similarly difficult obstacles and solved complex problems, it's easier to have hope about resolving the issues of today.

Sure, most of us were taught the outline of American history back in school; we know the basic storyline. But how many of us have read a detailed biography of Abraham Lincoln and know about his depression and complex personality? How many of us know about the behind-the-scenes peace negotiations after World War II and how they led to the fragile patchwork of nations that exists today in Europe and Asia?

History is our surest guide to a peaceful and successful future. Learning more about history is also great fun. Whether you read a great biography, watch a well-done documentary, or visit a historic landmark, studying our country's past can be as enjoyable as it is enriching. Here are some ways to keep history alive.

• Listen to recordings of the great speeches of the past century. Many are available for free if you have a computer. For example, at HistoryChannel.com, you can download real audio files of historic speeches; check out the site's "This Day in History" feature as well for other great audio and video clips. Also consider purchasing one of the fantastic CD box sets on the market, such as *The Greatest Speeches of All Time* or *Great Speeches of the 20th Century*. Spend an evening with Martin Luther King Jr., John F. Kennedy, Winston Churchill, or General Douglas MacArthur—without leaving home!

• Subscribe to *American History* magazine or *Military History* magazine for a monthly look at another era. There's no better way to know the past than by reading about the cultural, political, and social impact of our forefathers.

• Take a field trip. Make a point of going to the historical museums in your area. Whether it's the Erie Canal Museum, the Pony Express Museum, or the Sioux Indian Museum, there's bound to be an exhibit worth exploring near you. Historical museums aren't just for elementary school students; they're for the entire community, preserving history for all of us. Or try a walking tour of your city or village. You may discover that your hometown was the site of more than just your childhood; find out what battles were waged there, what institutions were built, and which ghosts still lurk about.

- SIXTY-EIGHT -

Define Your Terms

There was a time in America when the words
liberal and *conservative* weren't mean-spirited
political epithets, and *skeptical* wasn't used to describe
an unpatriotic or negative attitude.

But in today's contentious world, politicians, television com-
mentators, and even newspaper reporters often misuse
language to obscure an issue, score a point against an oppo-
nent, or create superficial and unfair labels.

The problem is, when it becomes difficult to discern a properly
used word from a well-spun stereotype, conversation breaks
down. Rather than critiquing an idea on its merits, we judge it
by the category in which the spin-masters place it ("Oh, that's
just the conservatives' position!").

What to do? Become your own master of words. Keep a dictionary in the living room and look up words that dominate
our national conversation or that seem out of place in an article

or misused on TV. Being able to parse intellect from invention will make you a wiser and more potent member of the democracy. Asking questions about what you read or hear may just lead you out of the doublespeak and into the truth.

Speaking of which: Do you know the difference between cynicism and skepticism? The dictionary defines cynicism as:

... contemptuously distrustful of human nature and motives ... based on or reflecting a belief that human conduct is motivated primarily by self-interest ... PESSIMISTIC; implies having a gloomy, distrustful view of life.

Now take a look at the definition of skepticism:

an attitude of doubt or a disposition to incredulity either in general or toward a particular object ... the doctrine that true knowledge or knowledge in a particular area is uncertain ... the method of suspended judgment, systematic doubt, or criticism ...

How do you approach the world around you? Are you suspicious and distrustful, or do you look at matters critically and systematically? Try to recognize when cynicism may inappropriately cloud your judgment and when skepticism is the correct response to a speech, article, claim, or policy.

With a dictionary at your side, you may realize that certain "dirty" words aren't so bad and that most words are bipartisan! Here are a few more terms you may want to look up.

optimism/idealism
conservative/liberal
liberty/protectionism
partisan/bipartisan

- SIXTY-NINE -

Be a Good Patriot

America is a country of unprecedented freedoms, diversity, rights, and opportunities; a nation that is both a world leader and a safe harbor.

We should be proud of our great country and the potential it affords each of us lucky enough to live here—and no one should feel self-conscious about showing that pride. Put the American flag outside your home on holidays. Sing "The Star-Spangled Banner" with gusto at ballgames. Place bumper stickers on your car that show your love for your country, its national parks, its great monuments. Defend your country when cynics are ranting unfairly. This is what patriots do.

Always know the limits, though. Patriotism ceases to be a good thing when it is used to denigrate other people or cultures. Used as a weapon, patriotism is hurtful to both others and ourselves. Taken to its furthest extreme, patriotism is an excuse for terrorism.

Sometimes, even what seems like innocent patriotic zeal can cross the line. For example, the 2002 Winter Olympics in Salt Lake City were heavily criticized in the media and by the world community for being excessively nationalistic. The Olympics are meant to be a forum of global unity, with healthy competition among friendly nations and opportunities for athletes and spectators from throughout the world to mingle and enjoy each other as equals. It is the host country's job to provide a positive, open environment in which this can occur. However, critics contend—with some validity—that the 2002 Olympiad was marred by U.S. patriotism gone awry. National pride yielded to petty and demeaning chants and loss of respect for our guests from other countries.

When ethnocentrism is wrapped in the American flag, our culture suffers. That's why situations like the 2002 Winter Olympics matter. Rather than being seen as the good sports and openhearted people that we typically are, we were shown by the world media to be bad sports. That created the potential of fueling the ire of our enemies and frustrating our allies. And so we relearned an important lesson: The flag is a symbol of pride, not a weapon to be wielded or a vehicle for taunting.

This lesson applies in other arenas as well, particularly politics. The flag is not a statement of party affiliation or a symbol of political fervor. To fly a flag and be a patriot is to love your country—not to love an institution, a political party, or a piece of legislation. After all, in the immortal words of Benjamin Franklin, "Where liberty dwells, there is my country."

- SEVENTY -

Dream Big

What makes America different from totalitarian
states—indeed, from many other countries—is our
fierce individualism and thirst for adventure.

The American way is to achieve all you can in life. As a people,
we frown upon those without ambition, without a plan, without a dream, and we make heroes out of achievers, whether in
business, sports, leadership, science, or service. This is one of
the greatest attributes of our country. We don't measure people
by their lineage or the amount of money they inherited or the
education they've received. We measure them by what they
accomplish.

What is your passion? Have you had a secret goal since childhood? Do you have a list of things to do before you die? Then
it's time to renew your pursuit of those dreams. It's time to
commit yourself anew to the joys of accomplishment. Whether
you want to turn your dusty basement into a darkroom, attend

a Broadway show, or run with the bulls in Spain, your dreams have the power to fuel your zest for life. Realizing one dream may inspire you to pursue even larger goals, such as changing careers, and inspire your children to dream big as well.

Maybe you want to write the great American novel, take a master class at the American Ballet Theater, learn to make ceramics, or follow in the footsteps of Lewis and Clark. Whatever the dream, if you embrace the spirit of American adventure, you may be inspired to change the world. When citizens follow their dreams, America becomes a more imaginative and exciting place to live.

If everyday life or hard circumstances have dulled your dreams, don't despair. Start small and let them grow. Here are some ambitions and challenges that may spark your interest.

- Learn to sail
- Make a quilt
- Go on a whale watch
- Take a zero-gravity flight and experience weightlessness
- Create a model-train room in your house
- Go skydiving
- Attend clown school
- Hike into and out of the Grand Canyon
- Visit the country your ancestors came from
- Take a class at the local college
- Teach a class at the local college
- Take French cooking classes
- Run a marathon

Take on a Year of Service

There are important ways to contribute to your country throughout the course of your everyday life, but why not do something really bold and devote a year to serving America? It may seem impossible, but it's more achievable than you may think. How? Consider making your first year of retirement a year of service.

These days, retirees are healthier, fitter, and more active than ever, so kick off the next chapter in your life with a year of service. By working abroad, you can represent America to other cultures with warmth, vigor, and compassion. By working here at home, you can help the next generation learn the importance of giving back. Seniors have experience and knowledge gained during lifetimes of running businesses, raising families, teaching children, and acquiring unique job skills. There is perhaps no person better suited to go out into the

197

world for a year of service, fun, and new life experiences than a new retiree.

There are lots of opportunities across America and the world for willing seniors. Whether it's serving as a mentor in an inner city, a nurse in a needy country, a legal aid adviser on a Native American reservation, an AIDS counselor in Africa, or just as a helping hand in your neighborhood library, you will be able to find a program that suits your needs and experience. Look into service as the first part of your retirement goals—you could wind up having the adventure of a lifetime!

Check out the following organizations for great opportunities for senior service and adventure.

- **Senior Corps.** Like AmeriCorps, Senior Corps (SeniorCorps.org) will place adults over 55 in service opportunities in communities throughout the United States.

- **Peace Corps.** This American service institution (PeaceCorps.gov) is still the standard for amazing volunteer experiences abroad—no matter what your age.

- **Habitat for Humanity.** After Hurricane Katrina and the South Asian tsunami, Habitat for Humanity (Habitat.org) is busier than ever and is always on the lookout for volunteers.

- **Global Service Corps.** Global Service Corps (GlobalServiceCorps.org) places people of all ages on special volunteer projects for two weeks to six months.

- **United Planet.** U.P. (UnitedPlanet.org) emphasizes cultural exchange and diversity to create a "community beyond borders" for people of all ages.

- SEVENTY-TWO -

Visit Our Country

For too many of us, the only way we experience America's great cities and landscapes is by watching television. While it's easy to get stuck at home because our hectic lives and many responsibilities crowd out thoughts of travel, one of the most wonderful contributions you can make to America is simply to enjoy it.

We live in one of the largest and most majestic countries in the world, with nine time zones, coasts on two oceans, arctic winters up north, tropical summers down south, historic cities, national parks, and natural wonders unlike those anyplace else on Earth. Take advantage of all that the United States has to offer and teach your children about our great country along the way. Besides, your tax dollars have already paid for many museums, parks, interstate highways, nature preserves, and landmarks. Why not get out there and see where your money went?

Make it a ritual: once every other year, say, take a three- to five-day trip to a part of America you haven't visited before. Here are some ideas to get you started.

• Spend several days in each of America's most beloved national parks, such as the Grand Canyon, Yellowstone, Acadia, the Everglades, or Yosemite.

• Then find your way to the less visited but equally magnificent national parks: Shenandoah, Sequoia, Zion, Bryce Canyon, Hot Springs, Olympic, and more.

• Visit our nation's capital, Washington, D.C. Tour the White House and the Library of Congress, stop at the war memorials, immerse yourself in the Smithsonian museums, and meet the pandas at the National Zoo.

• Go to the Alamo in Texas and learn about one of our nation's greatest battles, or do the same at Gettysburg in Pennsylvania.

• Hike the Appalachian Trail (or part of it, anyway!).

• Visit a historic first city like Philadelphia or Boston—check out the Liberty Bell and eat a cheese steak or throw some tea into the harbor and wolf down some clam chowder.

• Go to New York City and find out why it remains one of the world's favorite cities. Catch a Broadway show, go to the Statue of Liberty, dance in Times Square, enjoy its world-class museums, and sample its amazing mix of music.

• Drive through the Rocky Mountains in autumn, then, on your next trip, do the same in the Green Mountains of Vermont.

• Check out the Pacific Northwest. Sift for gold, go fly fishing, and savor a cup of coffee in beautiful Seattle.

- Rent a convertible and cruise across Route 66.
- Drink mint juleps in Savannah, Georgia, and take a ghost tour.
- Take a pottery class in Santa Fe, New Mexico.
- Listen to the blues in Chicago.
- Lose yourself in the open spaces of Minnesota, Montana, or North Dakota.
- Visit the Rock & Roll Hall of Fame and Museum in Cleveland.
- Take a train trip through the South or ride the famous steam train from Durango to Silverton, Colorado.
- Drive one of the world's most magnificent coastal roads, the Pacific Coast Highway in California. Along the way, stop and tour one of our country's most amazing residences, the Hearst Castle.

The list goes on and on and on. For tons more ideas for you and your family, check out America's Byways at Byways.org. Nothing will make you appreciate your country more than experiencing it firsthand.

- SEVENTY-THREE -

Embrace the Past,
Live for the Future

Each of us has a time that we cherish as a Golden Age,

not just for ourselves but also for our country.

For millions of young Americans, that special time

is occurring right now.

While many older Americans may consider today a time of information overload and intolerably high-speed living, our younger citizens will someday recall the year 2006 as their most innocent time. We just love nostalgia in this country; it permeates every aspect of our arts and culture, willing us to believe that "then" was happier and less stressful than "now." Of course, there's nothing wrong with waxing nostalgic for great moments long gone, but being wistful for the endless summer of yesterday is a whole lot different from decrying the end of the good years for America—which, for some reason, many of us do.

To be sure, our recent history is as vivid and alive as our memories, which is why we are so expert at romanticizing our pasts. But America is not merely one generation; we are all eras at once. Today's America is comprised of a medley of experiences and ages. We are the Greatest Generation; we saved the world from evil, forged a new economy, and created a stronger nation with straightforward values. We are the Baby Boomers; we engendered social change, pioneered the Civil Rights Movement, and swayed to the rhythms of Woodstock. We are Generation X; we grew up in the Me Decade of the 1970s and the indulgent 1980s, rediscovered angst, and devoted entire cable TV channels to preserving our youth. And now we are the Millennials; we are the most technologically sophisticated and socially tolerant generation the United States has ever seen. We are all of these people right now, and we will be so much more.

This is a country that for 230 years has ceaselessly adapted and improved. We have weathered wars, economic depressions, periods of misguided righteousness, civil unrest, and repeated massive influxes of new immigrants. But however trying the struggles our country has faced, it has always been the people who continually rose to the challenge. Our success as a nation is ultimately the success of its people. Not the Senate, not the House of Representatives, not even the president. It is the American people who have grasped the incredible promise of these United States and forged a democracy more vibrant and diverse than our Founding Fathers could have imagined.

About the Charities

In gratitude for their support, the Reader's Digest Association will donate a portion of the proceeds from the sale of *For America* to charities selected by Presidents Bush and Clinton.

Acknowledgments

As with most great service projects, this book is the result of efforts by a number of amazing people. *Reader's Digest* magazine, where I work as a senior editor, has been wonderful to me. I'd like to thank Jacqueline Leo, editor in chief, for this remarkable opportunity and for her invaluable guidance. William Beaman, Washington bureau chief, has my eternal gratitude for his ceaseless good cheer, wise advice, and precise editing. The entire editorial staff at *Reader's Digest* deserves plaudits, but a few should receive special mention: Alexis Mitchell, John Mitchell, Ed Goralski, Ann DiCesare, Deirdre Casper, Susan Doremus, Andrew Simmons, and Maureen Mackey. Thank you also to Maura Mahoney, who provided invaluable research in record time. The whole team at Reader's Digest Books has my utmost appreciation. And, finally, no one helped me more through this process than the inimitable Neil Wertheimer, who showed patience, boundless creativity, and humor, all while sharpening my words and keeping me lucid! He also taught me that a book is a symphony and a collaboration—one I would gladly repeat.

My Washington, D.C., brain trust was crucial to writing this book. Thank you, Amy Sullivan, Matt Gaffney, Jonathan E. Kaplan, Kate Marsh, Spencer Ackerman, Tucker Reilly, Eric Columbus, Paul Ghosh-Roy, and especially Erica Hoffmann, who took brainstorming to heretofore unrealized heights. I'd also like to spotlight my two favorite volunteer organizations: Project Otzma, which gave me a community service fellowship in Israel that changed my life, and the Washington, D.C.–based College Bound program, which embodies the message of this book. Thank you, Jamaal Morgan, for reminding me how bright the future can be. Thank you to my family: my mother the passionate teacher, my father the sage counselor, and Deb and Shiloh, who bring huge hearts to every project they tackle. Finally, thank you, J. Peter Scoblic, whose hopes for our country and ardent patriotism are palpable. You make it possible to take on great challenges, to strive for character, to laugh unreservedly, to follow the big dreams.

SACHA ZIMMERMAN

DATE DUE
